ESSAYS ON CULTURAL TRANSMISSION

ESSAYS ON CULTURAL TRANSMISSION

MAURICE BLOCH

LONDON SCHOOL OF ECONOMICS MONOGRAPHS ON SOCIAL ANTHROPOLOGY

Volume 75

Oxford • New York

First published in 2005 by
Berg
Editorial offices:
1st Floor, Angel Court, 81 St Clements Street, Oxford, OX4 1AW, UK
175 Fifth Avenue, New York, NY 10010, USA

© Maurice Bloch 2005

Berg is the imprint of Oxford International Publishers Ltd.

Library of Congress Cataloging-in-Publication Data

Bloch, Maurice.
Essays on cultural transmission / Maurice Bloch.
    p. cm. — (London School of Economics monographs on social
anthropology ; v. 75)
    Includes bibliographical references and index.
    ISBN 1-84520-287-2 (pbk.) — ISBN 1-84520-286-4 (cloth)
  1. Ethnopsychology. 2. Cognition and culture. I. Title. II. Series.

    GN502.B54 2005
    155.8'2—dc22

                                                      2005010965

British Library Cataloguing-in-Publication Data

A catalogue record for this book is available from the British Library.

ISBN-13 978 1 84520 286 6 (Cloth)
              978 1 84520 287 3 (Paper)

ISBN-10 1 84520 286 4 (Cloth)
              1 84520 287 2 (Paper)

Typeset by JS Typesetting, Porthcawl, Mid Glamorgan
Printed in the United Kingdom by Biddles Ltd, King's Lynn

www.bergpublishers.com

CONTENTS

ACKNOWLEDGEMENTS

'Why trees, too, are good to think with: towards an anthropology of the meaning of life' originally appeared in Laura Rival (ed.), *The Social Life of Trees: Anthropological Perspectives of Tree Symbolism* (1998), and is reprinted here by permission of Berg Publishers.

'Questions not to ask of Malagasy carvings' originally appeared in Ian Hodder (et al.), *Interpreting Archaeology: Finding Meaning in the Past* (1995), and is reprinted here by permission of Routledge Publishers.

'Commensality and Poisoning' originally appeared in *Social Research* 66(1): 133–49, and is reprinted here by permission of the Graduate Faculty of Political and Social Science at the New School University.

'What is passed on from parents to children: A cross-cultural investigation' originally appeared in the *Journal of Cognition and Culture* 1(1): 43–68, and is reprinted here by permission of Brill Academic Publishers.

'A well-disposed social anthropologist's problems with memes' originally appeared in Robert Aunger (ed.), *Darwinizing Culture: the Status of Memetics as a Science* (2000), and is reprinted here by permission of Oxford University Press.

'Are religious beliefs counter-intuitive?' originally appeared in Nancy K. Frankenberry (ed.), *Radical Interpretation in Religion* (2002), and is reprinted here by permission of Cambridge University Press.

'Kinship and evolved psychological dispositions: the mother's brother controversy reconsidered' originally appeared in *Current Anthropology* 43(5): 723–48, and is reprinted here by permission of the University of Chicago Press.

PREFACE

This book consists of a mixture of unpublished work and articles which have already been published, often in somewhat inaccessible places. By bringing these pieces together, it attempts to characterize a particular approach to anthropology which, in many ways, goes against the grain of contemporary fashion.

Recent Anthropology has excelled in giving fine interpretative accounts of different groups of people from around the world but, by contrast to earlier periods, it has shied away more and more from linking these ethnographic accounts to wider theoretical issues. By contrast, theoretical works, especially those dealing with the relation of the cognitive sciences and anthropology, seem to have gone the other way. These have used ethnography only in passing, merely as brief illustrations of much more general points. By contrast, most of the material gathered in this book is inspired by the attempt to bring together the ethnographic experience of a fieldworking anthropologist with his much more fundamental considerations about the place of cognition within the historical process.

For me, fieldwork in a remote setting is as much a matter of obtaining data as an intellectual discipline aimed at bringing the theoretician back down to earth and as a defence against the exoticization which occurs when we are away for long periods from direct contact with the people we study. Fieldwork forces us to remember the complexity of human life and to correct the inevitable tendency to believe that introspection, carried out in tranquillity from the embedded position of our own particular culture and society, is straightforward.

The kinds of question which I try to answer in these chapters are often initiated by reflections on how to interpret behaviours observed during fieldwork. Indeed they are often the continuation of reflections which began as I was living in that small isolated village in the Eastern forest of Madagascar where most of my recent fieldwork has been carried out. Inevitably, such interpretative work also begins with introspection, but carried out when one is embedded in another culture. This is a method which is also fraught with dangers, but it cannot, for all this, be abandoned. Precisely because of my awareness of these dangers, I use what I know of the cognitive sciences to theoretically criticize my impressions and so advance my understanding of what I observe. Thus, in these study the questions begin with ethnography and lead to theory. This is the case for Chapters 2, 3 and 4.

Chapter 5 is similar but also different. The continual questioning of the ethnographic data in the light of cognitive theory which characterizes the work presented in this book has sometimes made me dissatisfied with the nature of the evidence produced by the largely traditional anthropological methods I have usually utilized in the field. This dissatisfaction made me go back to studying the same phenomena, in this case ideas surrounding heredity, in a different way. Thus, working in the Malagasy locality which I have been studying for more than thirty years, together with the help of the psychologists Susan Carey and Gregg Solomon, I tested the developing understanding of the nature of physical and cultural transmission between parents and children in a way which would be more familiar in psychology. The preliminary results of the study presented have provided the basis for a much more rigorous and much wider ranging study by Professors Astuti, Carey and Solomon. This was to yield anthropologically spectacular new results (2004).

Chapters 6, 7, 8 and 9, by contrast, begin with theoretical questions which have been prominent in recent discussions concerned with the relationship of cognition and anthropology. Yet, in spite of the difference in presentation, these too are characterized by the fact that I approach these topics as a fieldworking anthropologist. This is even true of Chapter 9 which is the result of a co-operative enterprise which attempts to integrate the very general theoretical framework proposed by Sperber and central anthropological concerns.

Finally, Chapter 1 is of a completely different character. Originally given in a somewhat modified form as an Inaugural lecture at the Free University of Amsterdam, it attempts to explain why, from a non-specialist perspective, there is ample justification and a need for the kind of generalizing anthropology to which all the chapters of this book contribute.

REFERENCE

R. Astuti, G. Solomon and S. Carey. 2004. *Constraints of Conceptual Development*. Monographs for the Society for Research in Child Development, no. 277.

CHAPTER I

WHERE DID ANTHROPOLOGY GO? OR THE NEED FOR 'HUMAN NATURE'

Maurice Bloch

I was recently asked the question: 'Where did anthropology go?' by a psycholinguist from a famous American university. She was commenting on the fact that she had tried to establish contact with the anthropology department of her institution, hoping that she would find somebody who would contribute to a discussion of her main research interest: the relation of words to concepts. She had assumed that the sociocultural anthropologists would have general theories or at least ask general questions, about the way children's upbringing in different cultures and environments would constrain, or not constrain, how children represented the material and the social world. She was hoping for information about exotic societies and about those groups which she had already learned should not be called primitive, but that is what she meant. She was hoping that her enquiry about a topic that is inevitable in any discussion about culture would be equally central to the three disciplines of psychology, linguistics and anthropology, and would therefore be an ideal ground for constructive co-operation, that is, one where the different parties could articulate and challenge the theories on which their different disciplines are built.

In fact she found that nobody was interested in working with her, but what surprised her most was the hostility she perceived, caused not only by the suggestion that cultural social anthropologists were interested in simple exotic societies, but even more by the idea that they might be interested in formulating and answering general questions about the nature of the human species or that their work could be compatible with disciplines such as hers.

The lack of any generalizing theoretical framework within which her research interest might find a place is not surprising when we look at what kind of thing is done in many university departments under the label social or cultural anthropology. Take for example the interests listed on the web site of the anthropology department of the University of California at Berkeley (which incidentally is not where our psycholinguist came from). Here are some:

> *Genomics* and the anthropology of modernity, Science and reason, The anthropologies of education, law, tourism, Food and energy, space and the body, Post-soviet political discourse, Violence, trauma and their political and subjective consequences, Social and cultural history, (Post) colonialism, Social mediation of mind.

I do not intend here to criticize the value of the studies which lie behind these titles. In fact, I know that many are excellent and interesting, but one need not be surprised that our psycholinguist got so little response to her request for a coherent body of theories from anthropologists. What possible core of shared questions and interest could departments of this sort have to which her interest might then be related?

This incoherent fragmentation, in any and every direction, so long as the topics will find favour with funding bodies and seem relevant to the concerns of the moment, makes the existence of anthropology departments as working units difficult to justify intellectually. Indeed, this is what Eric Wolf already complained about shortly before his death, and led to the near destruction of anthropology at Stanford University.

But are we dealing simply with a problem internal to the ways in which universities function, simply an accidental result of the way the discipline has evolved in the academy, yet another illustration of the inevitable arbitrariness and shift of boundaries within science? The frustrated hope on the part of our psycholinguist that she could obtain guidance to her questions from professional anthropologists might indeed seem a rather limited problem of communication within modern universities where, after all, it is common for people from one discipline to misunderstand the nature of another.

I shall argue here that there is much more at stake, because the negative response to our psycholinguist's request for a discipline, such as what anthropology might reasonably be expected to be, is far from an arcane missed appointment, internal to the cloistered world of academia.

Let us consider a very different situation.

One evening, in early 2004, I was doing fieldwork in the little village of Ranomena. This is a place deep in the Malagasy forest, cut off from all modern means of communication and only reachable on foot. I was sitting in near total darkness in the tiny house of the family who have been my hosts, on and off, during several periods of field study, scattered over almost thirty years. The evening meal had been eaten and consequently the fire had burned down. This was, as is usual at this time, a rare moment of relaxation and reflection, in which I joined freely. The conversation soon turned, as it often did, to questions of a philosophical nature, though it had begun in a less general way. People had been imitating, remembering and making fun of the accents and the vocabularies of other ethnic groups in the huge and culturally very varied island of Madagascar. The people of the village, the men at least, are experts in linguistic and cultural diversity since, when they are young and vigorous, they go as wage labourers to many different parts of the country, where they work for several months at a time as woodcutters or carpenters, and where they are often employed by merchants originating from different parts of the Indian subcontinent. After many anecdotes about the linguistic variations they had encountered on their travels, the conversation rapidly took on a more theoretical turn. If people used different words, did they understand the phenomena they designated so differently in the same way? If we are all related, how had this variation come about? Were the speakers of unrelated languages fundamentally different types of moral beings? And if they were, as some maintained, was this due to the language they had learnt, or was the language the manifestation of a deeper cause? In order to grapple with this problem the discussants proposed a thought experiment. What about the children of those Malagasy who had emigrated to France and who only spoke French? Were they in any sense really Malagasy in their social morality, in their ways of thinking and working and in their emotions? Would their skin be whiter than that of their parents? And, if not, as everybody seemed finally to agree, if they came back to live in Madagascar, would their dark skin mean that they would learn Malagasy more easily than, for example, I had, or the children of Europeans? Thus the question of what is learnt and what is innate was formulated and reformulated in many, often completely abstract, forms.

The seminar continued.

If there was so much variation and mutability, could one say that all humans were one species or several? Were there discontinuities in racial and cultural variation or only a continuum? If we were all one family and, at bottom, all thought alike, how could it be that the histories of different groups of mankind had been so dissimilar and had given rise to such differences in technological knowledge and wealth? Why were the people from overseas, which the people of Ranomena tend to consider all much of a muchness, continually fighting, when they, by contrast, were all so peaceful? And, given that there is only one God (it is a Catholic village), how could it be that in the world there are people like the Hindus who do such completely exotic, unthinkable things as burning their dead?

These were the questions I recorded in just one evening, but these and other related ones are a familiar feature of intellectual life in Ranomena. People argue among themselves over these matters, whether I am there or not. However, because I was there, and because by now, after much explaining, the villagers of Ranomena have some idea of the kind of subject I teach, they turned to me for advice and expertise. After all, as they often tell me, I had seen and read about many more different people in the world than they had, I had studied long and hard and had gathered in myself the wisdom of many other knowledgeable people who had been my teachers. So, what could I say about these crucial questions? Well, I answered as best I could. But, what strikes me most clearly, as I reflect on such pleasant and interesting evenings, is that my co-villagers, in spite of their lack of formal education, were coming to the subject of anthropology with much the same questions as we might expect from anybody who turns to our discipline in a country such as Britain, whether as students, as readers of learned publications, or as practitioners of other disciplines in the academy. Indeed, as you may have noted, the very same question was being asked by the psycholinguist of people who call themselve anthropologists as did some of the Malagasy villagers.

The point I want to stress through these anecdotes is that there is a widespread, perhaps universal, demand for a subject such as anthropology and that this demand exists irrespective of culture, degree of education and intellectual tradition. People ask these questions of anthropologists because anthropology would seem to be the kind of discipline which might provide answers. It is to get answers to questions such as those that preoccupied the villagers of Ranomena, that people in Britain, or indeed anywhere, choose to study anthropology.

But, had the villagers of Ranomena actually penetrated the portals of the academy, would they have to face the same disappointment as our psycholinguist? The answer is probably yes. And, in order to understand how and why this state of affairs has come about, I attempt here an extremely brief overview of the academic history of the discipline. One, which will inevitably involve gross oversimplification and will ignore many counter-currents and eddies. I want to understand how and why the anthropology which others seek is becoming absent from anthropology departments. I want to argue that it is this absence which makes interdisciplinary co-operation and disciplinary coherence impossible.

The late nineteenth century was a time when a number of highly influential anthropological books were published. These purported to give a general account of the history of humanity in terms of general evolutionary laws. Thus, general characteristics of human beings were seen to be the cause of human history, which, therefore, had a necessary and unilineal character. These types of book were not new, but what was new was the fact that these general accounts were to be supported by a scientific research enterprise, the aim of which was to collect empirical evidence in support of the different theories. This became the justification for setting up university chairs and ultimately whole departments of anthropology in many European and American countries; indeed, this was the case at LSE.

The discipline was to operate a bridge between the history of life, up to the emergence of *Homo sapiens*, the subject matter of zoology, and the history of mankind, from the invention of writing, by which point historians could take over. Evidence to account for what had happened during this gap was to come from the four fields approach, still evident in many contemporary anthropology departments in the United States. The four-fields were archaeology, biological anthropology, linguistics and what became social and cultural anthropology.

The role of social or cultural anthropology in this schema was to provide evidence for the reconstruction of the history of mankind through the study of primitive people. The study of these people was relevant because of a familiar, but fundamental, assumption. The different groups of mankind advanced along a single necessary line of progress, from one stage to another. Technological or intellectual advances were the driving force for forward movement, but this was along a road which was traced by the internal potential of a shared human nature. The itinerary regarding politics, kinship, religion, morals and anything else, was thus universal and what varied was how far different groups had got pushed along. This being so it followed that finding a living contemporary group of people using a certain type of primitive technology, for example hunting and gathering, a study of their political organization, their kinship system, their religion, and so on, would yield information about the politics, kinship, religion and morals of our distant ancestors at the time when they had reached the same point along that single road. By this means, anthropology could discover the immaterial aspects of the life of those forebears whose material prehistory was being only gradually revealed by archaeology.

This general method was shared by most anthropological accounts of the time, although, of course, the evidence produced in this way was far from clear and, therefore, a number of competing accounts of the early history of mankind were produced. All these, however, shared an amazing confidence in the ability of the subject and its methods to fulfil the vast programme which it had outlined for itself. These theories are usually described as evolutionist or more precisely as unilineal evolutionist theories, and they all rest on a largely unexamined and simple notion of human nature which it was the purpose of the subject to flesh out.

The period about which I have been talking may be referred to as that of the founders of anthropology. It produced an ordered image of the history of mankind and of cultural and social variation. It is because of this that, in many ways, it was the heyday of anthropology's popular success.

Consequently we may consider what happened next as its twilight. In fact, there is not one but two accounts to be told about this subsequent history of the dimming of the evolutionist light. The first concerns the reputation among anthropologists of this moment of confidence in their subject and the other its reputation in the wider world beyond.

Very shortly after its establishment, evolutionist anthropology was destroyed by an obvious but fundamental criticism, which took very different forms but is always ultimately based on the same objection.

This is usually called the theory of diffusionism. I shall use the term here much more widely than is usually done to stress the fact that, in spite of superficial differences, we are always dealing with the same point. Thus I include under the term 'diffusionism', such trends as Geertzian culturalism and 'postmodernism' which all rest on the same foundation. The basic point of diffusionism – the basic objection to evolutionist anthropology – is that human culture does not proceed along a predetermined line, following a limited number of ordered stages. This is because human beings have the ability to learn from each other and can then pass on acquired traits through communication. This enables them to further build, transform, modify and combine what others have learnt and passed on to them. It is thus possible to argue, perfectly validly, if somewhat simply, that it is human contacts and thus ultimately history which, in great part, make people what they are, rather than their 'nature'. For the diffusionists it is not fundamental essential characteristics of human beings that explain history but the accidents of whom we are with and have been with. Unlike animals to whom evolutionary laws apply and who are, in the long term, determined by their biological inheritance, humans, for their part, are determined by other individuals; in other words, they are determined by culture.

The implications of focusing on the ability of humans to imitate and borrow information and then to pass it on to another by non-genetic means is genuinely far-reaching. It is what makes culture possible. Since people borrow cultural traits one from another, they can individually combine bits and pieces from different individuals. It follows that there are no naturally distinct social or cultural groups, tribes, peoples, etc. And since these combinations arise from anywhere, anybody and in any order, there are no general predictable laws of history. Because, unlike other animals, humans can transmit acquired characteristics across and within generations, the history of culture becomes an entangled, disordered, infinitely complex mess, quite unlike the ordered procession envisaged by the evolutionists. And since the past was this tangled directionless web, so will be the future; therefore it cannot be predicted. Thus diffusionist theory, by emphasizing a fundamental aspect of the species, seemed at the same time to have done the opposite – that is, to remove internal human nature as the determinant source of what happens in history and to replace it by factors which are external. It is as though the ability of humans to communicate and to pass on what they have learnt to others made all innate natural capacities irrelevant to the study of human history. A point of view exemplified in Geertz's uncharacteristically bad-tempered and sarcastic lecture 'Anti Anti Relativism' (Geertz 1984).

Diffusionism was, therefore, made to seem a knock-out blow against the original ambition of a science that was going to explain what had happened in human history in terms of a necessary evolutionary sequence. No subsequent theoretical criticism has ever had such an impact. Indeed, the point is so fundamental that it has simply been repeated ever since in many different forms. Talk of 'construction' in the social sciences is a reformulation of diffusionism, and the miasma (Hacking 1999) surrounding both ideas is the same. More particularly, the emphasis on the 'construction' of 'the individual' or 'the person' shows us where diffusionism always leads by means of a kind of theoretical slippage which I shall go on to discuss. Thus the work of such writers as Weber, Durkheim, Dumont, Foucault and many others is evoked again and again to 'unmask' the historical specificity of the notion of the 'Western individual', a point which is incoherently received to mean that the very existence of the study of human beings in general has somehow been made theoretically illegitimate.

Anthropology began by assuming that human history could be written as the natural history of human beings, as though we were an ordinary kind of animal whose behaviour was governed by the same kind of natural laws as that of other forms of life. This tenet was then apparently totally negated by the emphasis on culture, the product of constitutive communication, the producer of unpredictable historical particularities. Thus, unilineal evolutionary theory of human history was thrown out for a good reason, and a totally opposite view was proposed – one in which people are represented as infinitely variable creatures, constructed entirely by the whims of innumerable accidents of communication – came in by default. In a way reminiscent of antique dichotomies, animals were seen as constructed by nature and humans by their freed minds. It is laziness so often surrounding the words which led and leads to these outdated nature/culture debates since they can mean either simply that all humans act and live in the world in terms of representations which are culturally inflected, a totally obvious and unobjectionable point, or it can mean that these 'constructions' enable people to 'construct' the world they attempt to grasp as though this were formless plasticine, with mind which are equally able to entertain *any* old representation, a position which it would be impossible to defend were it ever to be examined.

However, in the fog of such imprecision, diffusionism/constructionism has meant that anthropology could not anymore have human nature as its subject because there was no such thing. Like history, social and cultural anthropology could then only be an assemblage of anecdotes about this and that. And this is, by and large, what it has become and what has produced the heterogeneous list of interests of the Berkeley Anthropology department. The contemporary situation seems therefore to be one where evolutionism has been dismissed and diffusionism has won, thereby leaving anthropology without the only centre it could have: the study of human beings.

This is well illustrated by the form of most contemporary anthropology teaching. At the risk of caricature, anthropology courses, whether introductory or more specialized, have in common the following general structure. They begin with a historical section, where the general theories of early anthropologists are explained. These may be from long ago, such as those of Boas, Durkheim, Westermark or Morgan, or more likely from the middle distance, Mauss, Radcliffe-Brown, Malinowski, Van Wouden, or Lévi-Strauss. Then, what is wrong with these theories is demonstrated, usually by means of ethnographic examples, and there the matter rests. Students are, therefore, left with a feeling of having little to say about the subject in general. They have lost a few misleading illusions in the process, which is all to the good; but, also, more insidiously, they have learnt that the very attempt to generalize – as the historical figures did – was, in and of itself, wrong. To be a good anthropologist thus seems to require to have learnt not to ask the questions which the Ranomena villagers, or our psycholinguist, ask.

This negative stance is not simply due to the way anthropology has developed within the academy. It is also due to the non-academic reputation of early evolutionary theories.

Ideas and publications proposing a unilineal evolution of human societies, going through a fixed number of stages, greatly antedates the academic anthropological evolutionists. But, probably, in part because these were so much in accord with their time, the works of the founders had an extraordinary contemporary influence, though often, somewhat indirectly, through such writers as Freud, Marx and several influential literary and artistic figures such as T.S. Eliot, Graves and Breton. The late nineteenth century and early twentieth was thus the period when anthropology, as an academic subject, although a very young academic subject, had an enormous impact on intellectual life. Since then, however, save for a few moments that, for a short time, seem to buck the trend, the general influence of contemporary anthropology has declined. The work of more recent anthropologists, especially those whose work has come out since the 1950s, with the possible exception of that of Margaret Mead on sex and Lévi-Strauss on structuralism, has had little influence on the main intellectual currents of the time.

On the other hand, outside anthropology departments, the influence of the founders of the discipline has continued unabated, distilled in various forms in the general culture in which we bathe. The idea of an evolutionary sequence of societies, customs, laws, religions, morals, extremely similar to that set out by the evolutionist anthropologists is still with us, even though sometimes a little disguised for the sake of political correctness. Thus, few people flinch at the implications of remarks such as 'It is particularly shocking to witness such brutality in the twentieth century and in an advanced country'. Even more surprising is the fact that books such as those of Tylor, Morgan or Frazer, which in their times sold far far more than any contemporary anthropology works, are still in print and still much read today, though not in anthropology departments. The reason for the continuing influence of these writers and the relative lack of influence of their successors is not difficult to find. It is simply that these early authors gave answers, however unacceptable, to the questions asked by the Malagasy villagers and by our colleagues in other disciplines, while more recent anthropologists have nothing to say.

The fact that professional anthropologists live in a world where explanatory theories they consider obsolete still dominate, while their own voices are little heard, has a reinforcing effect on the negative theoretical character of teaching. Every year university anthropologists are faced with new generations of students who have, or are imagined to have, consciously or unconsciously, absorbed anthropological evolutionist theories. Thus the teaching of anthropology is often envisaged by the professionals as an endless fight against erroneous doctrines held by the neophytes and which, ironically, were largely encouraged, if not created, by their discipline's forebears.

But there is yet a further element in the educational scene which influences anthropology and pushes it still further in this same direction.

Apart from the general impression that attempting to formulate general theories is a bad and obsolete habit, another message comes through, loud and clear, in the teaching of anthropology. One of the very bad things which the early anthropologists did was to have placed their own values above those of other cultures, thereby seeing the process of evolution as necessarily progressing toward peoples such as themselves and toward types of societies such as their own. It followed that those most unlike themselves were rude primitives of the very lowest order. To do this sort of thing is called ethnocentrism and is very wicked. Such a message is easily and well received by the kind of students who are likely to choose anthropology and who come from a world where the evils of racism and intolerance have been all too clear.

However, this rejection is far from unproblematic. When we look more closely, we find all kinds of elements treacherously merged with this notion of ethnocentrism. The charge that the evolutionist anthropologists were somehow revelling in the inferiority of those they chose to call primitives and that this legitimated violence against them is anachronistic and grossly unfair and, ironically, ethnocentric, since it ignores the context and language of their time. For example, Tylor, the founder of British anthropology, was very active in the anti-slavery movement and Morgan, the founder of American anthropology, was much involved in supporting Indian rights. Indeed, the real political involvement of the founders of anthropology contrasts with its absence on the part of many contemporary anthropologists who willingly loudly denounce evolutionism.

Also involved in the notion of ethnocentrism is the warning against seeing peoples with other cultures through the lens of our own values. In fact, two elements should be distinguished here. The first is a methodological point. It is an injunction to anthropologists that the task of interpretation requires as much as possible an effort of imagination. We must try to see others as though from their point of view in order to understand them. Few would quarrel with the benefits of such a stance. But, closely intertwined with this, is the idea that the avoidance of ethnocentrism is not just a matter of a temporary suspension of disbelief, but an absolute injunction, i.e., that we should never judge or evaluate others by the categories or standards of our culture or indeed by any standards at all. This proposal leads inevitably to moral and cognitive relativism.

Here I want to concentrate on the theoretical, or perhaps the rhetorical, problems involved in cognitive relativism. Cognitive relativism is often adopted without much theoretical scrutiny since it is based on a gut reaction to any attempt at generalization. Generalizations are felt to be nothing but mere products of the particular cultural configuration of the ethnographer, who is situated, as he or she inevitably is, at a given time in a given place. The demonstration that this is so is a source of great satisfaction to the profession as it demonstrates the superiority of anthropologists over lay people. What *they* think of at the bedrock of their ideas as being natural is shown to be but the shifting sand of a unique historical conjuncture in a unique location.

There is no doubt that this kind of criticism of much theory, especially social-science theory, is one of the major contributions that anthropologists have made to scientific enquiry. However, such a position can easily slip into a much more radical claim that any generalization, which will inevitably use an external basis for generalization, is always illegitimate because it will *always* be nothing but the projection of the anthropologist's way of thinking. This inevitably implies the idea that anthropology as a generalizing science about human beings is a mere illusion of particular cultures, or to put it another way, that the very idea of human beings as a subject of study is shown, once again, to be 'ethnocentric'.

We thus find ourselves in the present ridiculous situation. On the one hand when the question 'Is there a common human nature?' is asked, most people, although they probably will consider it rather silly, will answer without hesitation in the affirmative, but, on the other, anthropologists will very much want to answer no, but won't dare to, so they will just go into hiding. Perhaps, part of the reason for this embarrassment is that a straight negation, taken together with what being a member of an anthropology department would seem to mean literally, would imply arguing themselves out of a job.

Of course, denying the unity of mankind is not new in anthropology. However, those who previously advocated such a position, the so-called polygenists of the nineteenth century, argued that mankind was made up of unrelated species and consequently approved of slavery and the hunting of Australian Aborigines as though they were wild animals

(Stocking 1987). These might not be the precursors the present-day anti-anti-relativists would wish to claim.

The further surreptitious abandonment of a notion of human nature, involved in the condemnation of ethnocentrism in the dialectics of teaching, combines dangerously smoothly with the negative stance that the history of the subject has produced. These two elements therefore reinforce each other in an obscure way and produce the situation I described at the outset of this chapter, where, when faced by the kind of request of our psycholinguist, anthropologists, instead of attempting to respond, go into what looks like a silent sulk wrapped in an aura of self-righteousness.

Inevitably, the questioners, whether they are academic colleagues or Malagasy villagers, are less impressed with such a stance than the anthropologists would like them to be. And so, they simply go elsewhere to look for answers to their anthropological questions. And much is available, in the works of writers whose academic affiliations are very varied, but which I label here, for the sake of simplicity, as the new evolutionists. Thus, to mention only some of the most well known, we have Richard Dawkins, a zoologist, explaining kinship (1976), René Girard, a scholar of literature, expounding on the origin of religion (1972), Stephen Pinker, a psycholinguist, telling us about totemism (2002) and Matt Ridley, a scientific journalist, telling us about incest (2003). The impact of such works can easily be seen if we look at the sales of their books, a commercial success which contrast dramatically with that of my colleagues and my own. These books have sold in hundreds of thousands. In other words, they have had the same kind of diffusion as the work of Tylor, Frazer or Morgan had and they probably have a similar influence. The reason is not difficult to find: it is simply that these works seem to offer answers to the repeated questions of a public hungry for anthropology. The answer to the question 'Where did anthropology go?' is therefore to disciplines outside the social sciences where it is doing very well. In the meantime social and cultural anthropology departments, having lost their anchor in human nature, scrounge around for any odd topics, often already well studied in other parts of the academy, in the short-term hope of pleasing students and funding authorities.

We may well ask what is the reaction of professional anthropologists to the competition from those who seem to have taken over the anthropological core. The answer is almost none at all. They consider these new evolutionists theories with so much distaste that they seem to be almost unaware of their existence. Thus, most of my anthropological colleagues seem never to have heard of Dawkins's proposal about the nature of culture, or of the word *memes* which he had coined to express it, and if they have, they fail to know what it means. This is at a time when, if you type the word on Google you obtain 1,280,000 entries.

The point is that, not only do anthropologists not produce the same kind of works as those of Pinker or Dawkins, they also seem to have nothing to say about them. They have withdrawn from the fray to a place where they produce a large number of studies, some good, some bad, about this and that, without any guiding reason or without any attempt at building up a coherent body of knowledge. It is as though they consider the proposals made in this extra-disciplinary anthropology so beneath them that they are unwilling to acknowledge its very existence.

Part of the distaste of anthropologists toward such work is not simply arrogance; it is the feeling that they have seen it all before. Indeed, when we turn to the writings of these new evolutionists, we usually find exactly the same problems that anthropologists have demonstrated and denounced throughout the twentieth century in the work of the founders. For in the work of these writers we come across, for example, the old easy assumption that contemporaries with simple technology are fossils of an earlier age, that human groups form distinct empirical entities, that there are obvious and necessary connections between technology and such things as ancestor worship, etc.

Most fundamental of all, however, is the assumption that internal characteristics of human nature can be used directly to account for specific cultures and histories. It is a bit as if someone proposed to account for the pattern of motor traffic in London with an explanation of how the internal combustion engine functions. These writers are simply often repeats of the old evolutionists, although they sometime modify their position by according some place to particular cultures and historical conjunctures. But, in the end, these unique characteristics are represented as merely superficial, or hiding an unchanging and unchangeable universal base. The reaction of contemporary anthropologists then is to repeat the, up to a point, totally legitimate diffusionist points. It sometimes seems as though we were doomed to endlessly repeat the same confrontation between theories based on unacceptable and often superficial views of human nature, but which are nevertheless listened to, and non-theories which are little more than avoiding saying anything and which are therefore ignored.

But is this bind really necessary? I think not, and the first step in freeing ourselves from this endless to and fro is to note that the diffusionist/ evolutionist dichotomy, as it has been interpreted, carries with it quite unnecessary baggage. The evolutionists are believed to necessarily see human nature as a deterministic procrustean bed which makes particularistic history either impossible or a superficial irrelevance. The diffusionists talk as though they must replace evolutionist determinism with such immaterial disembodied phenomena as cultural traits and more recently symbols, representations and dialogues. Thus the diffusionist reaction to evolutionism bundles together a profound point about the nature of human beings, i.e., the revolutionary historical implications of the kind of brain possessed by *Homo Sapiens* with its ability to communicate and a quite different, and indeed contrary, usually totally unexamined, philosophical jump from materialism to the purest of idealism. An idealism which means that questions such as 'What are human beings like?' cannot even be approached. It is this idealism and its consequent refusal of a base to what we study which, first of all, leads to the incoherence of the subject and, secondly, to its inability to co-operate with other sbjects which are not similarly ashamed to be studying the phenomenon *Homo Sapiens*.

The point is really quite simple. It is essential that the implications of the continual transformation of people in the complex cumulative socio-historical process, best understood as complex communication, be made central, as indeed it was for the diffusionists. And, that consequently, we recognize that human history cannot be seen as the fulfilling of a once and forever given potential, which inevitably implies unilineality and predictability. But it is equally essential that the recognition of this central fact about people does not take us, in an absent-minded sort of way, to a place where people's bodies, minds and the world in which they exist have somehow vaporized.

And here, a third type of approach might help us, an approach in no way so fundamental as evolutionism and diffusionism, though it has sometimes pretended to be so. A position best thought of as a method, with a potential for theory, rather than a theory as such. I call this type of position functionalism, but again, as I did for evolutionism and diffusionism, I use the word in a wider and somewhat different manner than the way it is usually understood. Functionalism is a position that is not often given its due, partly because it was so clumsily and variously theorized. Also, I recognize and accept the often repeated and over-familiar criticisms that have been made against theories of self-proclaimed functionalists, such as is found in Radcliffe-Brown's and Malinowski's programmatic articles. These criticisms, however, only apply to extreme formulations, which, in fact, were never very significant for actual studies.

What I understand by functionalism is, above all, a commitment to seeing culture as existing in the process of actual people's lives, in specific places, as a part of the wider ecological process of life, rather than as a disembodied system of traits, beliefs, symbols, representations, etc. It is not accidental that such a position has developed together with the advocacy for long-term fieldwork and that it has waned with the latter's decline. This is because maintaining a focus on what has been rather misleadingly called the 'embodiment' of life processes is difficult away from specific and closely watched instances. Such a stance, therefore, requires a constant effort.

This is why functionalism, even in the very general sense in which I am using the term here, has been losing ground and why it has been replaced by various theories of the diffusionism/contructionism type. This lack of interest in functionalism is also probably due to the fact that it has been such a European stance which has been drowned by imported brassy theoretical American debates, the so-called science wars, endlessly stuck in the evolutionist/diffusionist controversy. However, the virtues of what I call functionalism are many.

Its strength lies in its insistence on the complexity of life in particular places and at particular times, on the fact that in normal practice the many facets of human existence, which other sciences, such as politics, philosophy, economics, art, agriculture, kinship, medicine, psychology and so on, separate for the sake of clarity and simplicity, are inextricably bound together. For functionalism the mental exists in the practical, and both are conjoined functions of bodies in the wider ecology of life.

Because of its insistence on local anchorings, functionalism cannot avoid facing frontally the particularism of human situations. In this it is like diffusionism and unlike evolutionism. However, it is not subject to diffusionism's idealism, since it insists on seeing ideas, representations and values as occurring in the natural world of action and transformation, of production and reproduction. It requires, therefore, a form of epistemological *monism,* uniting people and the environment, the mental and the biological, nature and culture. Thus, it also resists the dichotomies of some of the modern evolutionists, who, wanting to take into account the reality of culture, end up with a type of dualism which sees individuals as partly made up of an immutable universal base, and an essentially different superficial, cultural-historical superstructure.

Functionalism enables us to recognize the inseparable totality created by the particularisms of the specificity of human history *and* the properties of natural being in the natural world. It can therefore continue the difficult anthropological enterprise and pick up again the empirical and theoretical job of understanding an animal involved in history. This having been said, however, it is not difficult to foresee the difficulty such a position creates.

Quite simply, by taking so many things into account and refusing to separate them, because they are not separate, one risks finding oneself unable to say much except noting how complicated and interconnected everything is.

Functionalism is thus good at forcing us to look at the human world as it is and at forcing us to stop ignoring its unpredictable complexity. However, functionalism threatens to overwhelm by the complexity of the task it has set itself. This is because it is an attitude to theory rather than being a theory, though it has sometimes wanted to see itself as such. The functionalist is thus, in desperation, often tempted to give superficial quick-fix answers, as did Malinowski, at the end of his life, with his needs theory, or to take refuge in the mindless contemplation of ethnography for its own sake.

It may thus appear that, if we define our object of study as the unique human combination of unified biological and historical factors, the task of theorising is simply too enormous for our discipline. The point, however, is that, of course, it is. Theory cannot be about what is circumscribed by disciplinary boundaries – these are arbitrary though useful historical accidents, theory is defined by what it is about.

Let me return to the anecdote I began with. It concerned a psycho-linguist who wanted to work in co-operation with anthropologists because she believed that her knowledge of the development of language and conceptualisation in children could contribute to anthropological enquiry, while, for her part, she would gain from what we knew. In this chapter I have argued that the reason why such co-operation could not take place was the dogmatic and nevertheless largely unexamined refusal by anthropologists to accept that their ultimate aim is the study of human nature, the necessary core of their concerns and the point of contact between disciplines such as psychology and others, including ours, all concerned with humans, with minds and bodies living in natural environments. The refusal, however, is based on unexamined theoretical sleights of hand, abetted by aspects of the character of the teaching of the subject in the university.

However, if we accept what our subject cannot avoid to be about, then communication with many other scientific disciplines, also engaged in this same enterprise, becomes possible. Of course, interdisciplinary communication will still be difficult, but there need not be impassable theoretical partitions.

Indeed, in this grand alliance, the special appointed task of functionalist anthropology, with its continual insistence on the actual life of specific people in specific places, maybe, precisely, to link the different human sciences. These may be separated for good methodological reasons, but heuristic divisions always threaten to gain a false reality.

From such a perspective, contrary to what the evolutionists imagined, it becomes obvious that anthropology cannot pretend, by itself, to give answers to the questions which most people, including the Zafimaniry sitting around a dying fire deep in the Malagasy forest, quite rightly ask of our discipline. But this will not be a reason for avoiding these requests by disdaining them as do the diffusionist/constructionists. Rather, we will acknowledge that these questions are precisely what we should study together but with other disciplines concerned with the same phenomenon.

ACKNOWLEDGEMENT

I would like to thank R. Astuti, E. Keller and C. Stafford for helpful comments on an earlier draft.

REFERENCES

Dawkins, R. 1976. *The Selfish Gene*. Oxford: Oxford University Press.
De Martino, E. 1977. *La Fine del Mondo*. Torino: Einaudi.

Geertz, C. 1984. 'Anti Anti-Relativism', *American Anthropologist* 86: 263–78.

Gellner, E. 1982. 'Relativism and Universals', in M. Hollis and S. Lukes, *Rationality and Relativism*. Oxford: Basil Blackwell.

Girard, R. 1972. *La Violence et le sacré*. Paris: Grasset.

Hacking, I. 1999. *The Social Construction of What?* Cambridge MA: Harvard University Press.

Pinker, S. 2002. *The Blank Slate*. London: Allen Lane

Ridley, M. 2003. *Nature Via Culture*. London: Fourth Estate.

Schepper-Hughes, N. 1992. *Death without Weeping: The Violence of Everyday Life in Brazil*. Berkeley: University of California Press.

Sperber, D. 1982. 'Apparently Irrational Beliefs', in M. Hollis and S. Lukes, *Rationality and Relativism*. Oxford: Basil Blackwell.

Stocking, G. 1987. *Victorian Anthropology*. London: Collier Macmillan.

CHAPTER 2

WHY TREES, TOO, ARE GOOD TO THINK WITH

TOWARD AN ANTHROPOLOGY OF THE MEANING OF LIFE

Maurice Bloch

Trees are used as major symbols all over the world, and the purpose of this chapter is to present a tentative explanation of why this should be the case. The most obvious way of approaching this question is to consider what it is about trees and the way they are conceptualized that makes them such suitable objects for symbolization; and, indeed, this will be my concern. However, to do this, and to leave it at that, would be to forget what Victor Turner taught us (but also often forgot!): that ritual symbols are part of a process. It is not simply in the evocative capacity of the conceptualization of one of the objects concerned that we find an explanation of their presence at a particular stage in a ritual, but in their transformative potential during the process of ritual (Turner 1968). The ritual process is always focused on a special type of substitution, where one thing 'becomes' another, in the same way as wine 'becomes' the blood of Christ during the mass (Lévi-Strauss 1962: Ch. 8). These transformations are not arbitrary. When one thing is changed into another, it is clear that some sort of empirical connection between the two states still exists. It is this commonality that is to be the channel for the achievement of ritual. The famous flutes of Melanesian and South American rituals gain their power from the fact that the same material object, long and hollow, can be shared by something that is, at one moment, represented as a penis and, at another, as a vagina. Ritual transformations depend, therefore, on a connection that links different states, and on a difference sufficiently obvious to make the transformation worthwhile and arresting. Transforming wine into blood is typical of ritual; transformations of wine into whisky would not do. I view such transformative potential as the central fact of ritual symbolism, and shall argue here that the symbolic power of trees comes from the fact that they are good substitutes for humans. Their substitutability is due to their being different, yet continuous with humans, in that they both share 'life'. This distant commonality is intriguing, problematic and uncertain. Thus, both the shared element – life – and the uncertainty and distance between humans and trees must be considered and understood.

THE NEED FOR A GENERAL THEORY OF TREE SYMBOLISM

In *The Savage Mind*, Lévi-Strauss (1962) argues that animals are good as tools with which to think about human society, though his argument could – and does – apply to plants and many other things as well. According to him, this usefulness does not come from the nature of animals as such, but, rather, from the way they can be classified in contrastive sets and hierarchies that are then used to represent analogically socially and/or culturally created similarities and differences. He has been criticized by a number of anthropologists, who point out, in different ways, how, implicitly or explicitly, the uses of animal symbolism, including the critical contrasts that different cultures stress between species, are not arbitrary, as he suggests, but dependent on the recognition of what is known to be shared between animals and humans (Descola 1992). The point was that animals were good to think for humans because animals were alive in a way that was perceived to be similar to that of humans (Fortes 1972; Tambiah 1969), and because animals and people were ecologically linked in the food chain, as well as in other less obvious ways (Dahl and Hjort 1976).

Not only do all cultures seem somehow to recognize this kinship and mutual dependence between animals and humans, but some greatly dwell on it, and on the ethical problems it poses (Arhem 1996; Descola 1996; Karim 1981; Rival 1996). In the field of symbolism, the recognition of commonality and interdependence between people and other animals is not just a matter of mythical contemplation for human beings; it very often becomes also the very basis of certain ritual practices. In such rituals, what comes to the fore is the implicit unity of life: the fact that it involves such practices as eating, digesting and excreting, growing and withering, and, above all, being born and dying. Rituals thus exploit the parallels and connections established by the partly shared life processes of humans and non-humans in order to link dramatically the former with the latter. This is most often done through substitution and the subsequent killing of the animal, performed to bring about beneficial results for the human ritual partner such as, for instance, curing, renewal or even a form of immortality (Bloch 1992a).

If life and its processes are what are recognized as linking animals and humans, should this not also suppose an equal and similar role for plants in ritual and symbolism? In fact, a rapid survey of the comparative ethnography reveals that plants too are important, though, as Rival notes in her introductory chapter, they have rarely been the object of such theoretical interest and scrutiny as has been directed toward animals. Perhaps the reason is that the killing of plants in ritual, though it occurs (Rappaport 1968), is a less spectacular subject for ethnographic films than the essential staple of animal sacrifice that characterizes this form of entertainment. However, the general questions raised by the symbolic use of plants are just as interesting as those concerned with animals; indeed, they are similar, though not identical.

One such question comes from an observation that the use of plants in ritual forces on us even more strongly than does animal symbolism, i.e. that such use depends as much on the similarity plants are perceived to share with humans, as on the salient differences that clearly exist between these two kinds of living things. In the case of animal sacrifice, for example, similarities between animals and humans are usually used as starting points for practices that emphasize – even define – the gulf between people and other animate things. This is particularly true of rituals that stress that one species eats the other and not vice versa, or that one species has the ability to speak while the other does not (Bloch 1992a: Ch. 3). Thus animals may be sacrificed as substitutes for human beings precisely because they are both like and also fundamentally different from people. The ubiquity and repetitious nature of animal symbolism is to be explained by the fact that the same feature demonstrates a salient commonality between humans and animals, i.e. life, while the same differences between them are picked out from the limited list of possibilities that the real world offers to real people, among which lack of speech, promiscuous sexuality, edibility and lack of ancestors seem to be the most common. The basis of this type of symbolism therefore involves both the principles which govern the cognition of what living kinds have in common, and those that govern what differentiates them.

The same kind of argument can be made to apply to plant symbolism in general. The similarity stressed between plants and humans is basically the same as that between animals and humans, that is, the fact that both are alive, though, as we shall see, this common condition is somewhat less obvious when we are dealing with the vegetable world. The differences stressed are, however, totally different for plants and animals. For example, for plants the focus is often on rootedness. When we turn to that subsection of the vegetable world that we can loosely call 'trees', further, more specific, differences between them and humans become symbolically salient. In earlier articles on a group of Malagasy slash-and-burn cultivators called the Zafimaniry, who put extraordinary emphasis on the significance of trees, I showed how what was symbolically stressed about trees was the greater durability and hardness they display when compared with people (Bloch 1992b, 1993).

To be more specific, the Zafimaniry stress three types of connection between trees and people. First, that both are alive. Second, that humans rely on trees for: making houses; making the earth fertile and weed-free; producing heat for cooking and warmth; obtaining cash from outsiders by selling timber; and, last but not least, providing raw material for most artefacts and, as the Zafimaniry make a kind of bark cloth, even clothing. Finally, they stress that certain trees, because of their heartwood, have 'bones'. By contrast, in their symbolic representations, they emphasize four differences between trees and people: (1) the fact that trees and humans have different lifespans;[1] (2) the fact that trees transform themselves into a lasting material, wood, out of which durable artefacts such as houses can be made; (3) the fact that, although alive like animate beings, trees are immobile, and become fixed and associated with specific locations, in a way that is normally typical only of features of the landscape; and (4) the fact that the 'bones' of trees (by which is meant the lasting heartwood of the trunks) continue to increase as a proportion of the whole throughout the life of the organism, whereas the bones of people, once they have reached maturity, remain as no more than a small part of their bodies, and, indeed, seem to 'shrink' as they rot in the grave after death (Bloch 1992b). I have explained these ideas, and put them in the wider context of the general symbolism specific to the Zafimaniry, in a number of earlier publications. Indeed, with a degree of familiarity with the cultures concerned, it is relatively easy to give this kind of ethnographic, i.e. hermeneutic, interpretation of such local systems. To leave the matter there, however, as most contemporary anthropologists seem to want to do, is also, in a certain way, perverse. This is because the similarities of a system such as that of the Zafimaniry with many others cry out for more general explanations that are not tied to a single instance.

Anthropologists, nowadays, seem to have given up on any attempt to supply more general explanations, but this has simply led to other scientists trying to do so in their stead and, in the process, often repeating some of the discipline's past errors – errors that it has subsequently learnt to avoid. There is a need for anthropologists to go beyond particularities, since, as glancing over this book's contributions amply confirms, the same themes come up again and again all over the world. This, of course, does not mean ignoring the equally important fact that similarities between symbolic systems are accompanied by a fundamental variability that it would be methodologically misleading to forget. This is indeed a common situation in anthropology, and, for that matter, in other social sciences as well, where the realization of the co-presence of both obvious cross-cultural regularities and no less obvious cultural specificities has led to violent lurches between, on the one hand, theories that stress the irreducible particularities of specific cases, explicable only by a specific and unique history, and thereby forget the striking regularities across human cultures, and, on the other hand, theories that emphasize extra-cultural or extra-historical factors such as ecology, economy or constraints coming from the nature of human cognitive capacities, and that often, in the process, become ridiculously reductionist. However, it is in understanding the combination of (1) constraints coming from the world as it is, and as it presents itself as an opportunity for human production, together with (2) the particular cultural history of groups or individuals, and (3) the nature of human psychology, that we can begin to give reasonable epistemological accounts of our data. These may not always be achievable in practice, since, in many cases, the enterprise is impracticable, so that we are forced to give partial accounts, usually from a single one of these three perspectives. But if we do give such partial accounts, we must make the provisional character of our explanations clear, and present our explanations in such a way that they can be compatible, and 'wait for' combination with, the other two types of constraints. In other words, we must not construct theories that seem to exclude the recognition of either historical specificities or cross-cultural regularities. The remainder of this chapter is one such theoretical attempt. It looks at what might be the cognitive constraints that would explain cross-cultural recurrences in tree symbolism; but it does this in a way that 'awaits' combination with an ecological and a historical analysis.

COGNITIVE CONSTRAINTS ON TREE SYMBOLISM

The psychological literature on the cognition of plants offers a limited amount of choice from which to build theories that might explain recurrences in the symbolism of trees. In fact nowhere do psychologists or ethno-botanists begin to consider what is the central question of this chapter, i.e. what is it about such cognition that makes plants, and more specifically trees, particularly suitable for religious symbolism?

What we do have is relatively rich work on classification. The work of Brent Berlin and his associates (Berlin et al. 1973) has enabled us to discover important constants in plant and animal classification in different cultures. In particular, they have shown that living kinds tend to be ranked in terms of five ranks, though this does not include the overarching category of 'living kinds' itself, which seems to be taken for granted. They show that there is always a general level of classification for plants, although this may not be named, as is indeed the case for the Zafimaniry, and that trees are often an immediate subdivision of plants.[2] Implicit also in their work is an assumption that, as far as I know, has been unchallenged in both the psychological and anthropological literature, that all cultures, and therefore all people, have a concept of 'life'. Writers such as Berlin, and a number of subsequent psychologists, also argue that such classifications are anchored to a 'basic level', often resembling the scientific 'species level'. Finally, they stress that natural kinds, and especially living kinds, are thought of in terms of essences; that is, that people believe that below empirical features, such as colour, shape, smell or sound, there lies an essence that remains unchanged even if some typical empirical features normally associated with a particular species are lacking. Thus an albino leopard is still a leopard.

This point concerning the fundamental and universally unique way by which natural kinds and artefacts are conceptualized forms the basis of Atran's (1990) bold hypothesis that there is something innate about our cognition of living kinds, something that leads us to construct a specific 'living kinds' domain. To argue for a specific domain is to argue that a certain type of thought is relatively isolated from other types of thought, and that it is governed by principles of organization that are different from those applying to other areas of cognition. It is often argued, as in this case, that such a domain-specific module is invoked for dealing with a specific type of phenomena existing in the world. Atran then goes on to take two further, but not logically necessary, steps. First, that such a cognitive domain is governed by a distinct area in the nervous system. Secondly, that such an area is produced by a common human genetic heritage. Atran is therefore arguing, *inter alia*, that we have a dedicated device, the product of our genetic make-up, that enables us to recognize living things as such, to cognize them in a special and different way from, for example, artefacts, and to make presuppositions about them. Living kinds do not result from learned experience, but from innate human predispositions. One of Atran's main illustrations of this proposition is the essentialism with which species are understood. Thus everybody knows, that is, people in all cultures and all children after a certain age, that a tiger made to look like a lion is still, *really,* a tiger. It must also follow that, for Atran, all human beings in some way know and similarly understand what 'life' is, though he does not make this point explicitly.

Atran's work is very useful in two ways. First, it moves the discussion of classification away from a mere consideration of structure, toward a discussion of the cognitive processes by which classification is formed both ontologically and phylogenetically. Secondly, he, like a number of other authors, makes us reflect, not simply on the structure of classificatory systems, but also on the *way* living kinds are categorized. In particular, he stresses how living kinds always seem to be conceptualized as having a distinctive essence, which distinguishes them from other non-natural kinds. There are, however, a number of problems involved in Atran's approach, some of which concern his psychological theories, while others are of an anthropological nature. The anthropological objections are of three sorts. The first one is that in his enthusiasm to stress the universal features of classification systems, Atran underplays the very real and very great differences existing between cultures, between individuals, between adults and children, and between children of different ages. In fact, he seems to be at pains to discount all evidence for such variability. The second concerns the fact that, although he is more interested than most writers in the ethno-botanical field in the beliefs concerning the entities classified, he goes nowhere as far in this matter as most anthropologists would like; the folk ontology of people is only a small part of an anthropologist's concern, since she or he is mainly interested in how people use and speculate about different species. The third objection concerns the rigidity with which Atran imagines people's cognition. He seems unable to account for the tentative nature of so much of culture, for the degree of disagreement and doubt that is found in the field, or for the obvious significance of context.

The 'hardness' of his view of taxonomy is particularly significant here, since it is linked to one of the psychological problems implicit in his work. Atran, in his enthusiasm to stress the unique and universal understanding of living kinds, refuses the prototype theories of concepts initially developed by Eleonor Rosch, at least insofar as these theories apply to plant and animal kinds. This is because the prototype theory, with its emphasis either on best exemplars or on family resemblances, seems to negate the idea of an underlying essence. In order to criticize the prototype view of such concepts, Atran (1990: 55) is forced to move to a highly restrictive definition of folk classification, and even of *meaning*. One effect of these restrictions is not only to beg the question, since it only considers the 'meaning' of living-kind terms in relation to classificatory definitions, but also to exclude any possibility of understanding the ways in which the core meanings of concepts are exploited and extended that might explain the regularities observed in plant and animal symbolism.

It is the capacity of prototype theory to make us grasp the subtlety of the uses of concepts and their associated words in, for instance, metaphors, that has turned writers such as George Lakoff (1987) into supporters of this theory of the nature of concepts. Lakoff rightly stresses the value of this perspective for his own concerns. Atran, however, also has a point. There is now extensive evidence, both ethnographic and psychological, to show that adults, if not children as well, universally attribute something special and different to living things: that they possess an essential irreducible core. Such evidence cannot be ignored; but it cannot be all there is to the matter. If living kinds are as special as Atran argues, then it must also follow, either implicitly or explicitly, that what they have in common, i.e. *life itself*, must also be conceptualized. Atran's theory, like all other theories about living kinds, implicitly requires knowledge and understanding of life, even though the precise nature of this knowledge and understanding is rarely examined.

It is here that some recent developments in the work on concepts might come to our aid. A number of writers, among them Frank Keil (1992), have modified our view of concepts in general by stressing that, at least in the case of living things, concepts contain at their core implicit 'theories'. Such writers, in this way similar to those advocating the prototype view, are able to recognize both the looseness of concept extensions and the significance of their rich and unpredictable associative fringe, while still retaining the key element, stressed by Atran, that adults believe, rightly or wrongly, that there is a strong essential theoretical core to living kinds. Unlike classical concept theory, Keil's formulation defines this core, not in terms of empirical features, but in terms of 'theories'. When applied to living kinds, such formulations are problematic insofar as what is meant by 'essence' could refer to two entirely different sorts of things. It could simply concern the 'dogginess' of dogs, in which case the core theory would be about this 'dogginess'. Or, alternatively, the conceptualization could imply an understanding of living kinds as *living*, and a belief in an underlying essence. It would then be because dogs are *alive* that people believe that, in spite of their bewildering variety, they all share dogginess. In this case, the core theory is about life itself and in general, the essentialism of particular living kinds is a mere epiphenomenon. In other words, if living kinds are understood by adults, whether implicitly or explicitly, as 'living', then what we need to uncover is their 'theory of life'. It seems to me that both Atran and Keil are endorsing both the alternative positions outlined in the previous paragraph at the same time, without really distinguishing them. This is clearly unsatisfactory.

It is important to be clear that, for the purpose of this chapter, I am only concerned with the question raised by the second alternative, since, whatever the virtues or otherwise of the former, it is the latter position that seems well supported in both the anthropological and psychological literature. The key questions are: (1) What do lay people, implicitly and explicitly, understand by life? and (2) How can the nature of this concept help us to understand such phenomena as the use of plants in general, or trees in particular, in symbolism and ritual? Writers such as Atran or even Keil, who hardly discuss the concept of life itself, seem of little help in answering either of these two questions. They probably believe that the concept of life is not constructed, but innate, and that, consequently, little can be said about it in cognitive terms. Whether they are right in this is ultimately a matter for research; but, as we shall see, their position has not gone unchallenged in psychology.

From an anthropological viewpoint, the necessary corollary to the innatist hypothesis (that all human beings recognize unproblematically certain kinds as living and others as not living), is also suspicious. Anthropologists have shown that the way in which lay people seem to consider these matters is highly tentative, discursive and complex. I am not arguing against a writer such as Atran that the core concept of life is culturally variable. It seems to me that, on this matter, the ethnographic record backs him completely (Ellen 1996; Descola 1996). What is at issue is different. Both Atran and Keil stress the fundamental difference between living kinds and artefacts,[3] to such an extent that being alive or not is assumed to be a clear-cut issue. Atran (1990) is particularly extreme in this matter. On page 56, he tells us that in lay taxonomy 'every natural object is either a living kind or not', presumably for all people, at all times. The anthropological record contradicts such strong assertion; indeed, Atran himself admits that such objects as lichens and fungi are only doubtfully recognized as being alive by Itza Maya,[4] as they also are by the Zafimaniry, according to my own knowledge of the ethnography.

If we turn to the Zafimaniry and to the limited insight into concept-ualization that vocabulary provides, we see how difficult it would be to maintain an assertion such as that of Atran, and how what evidence there seems to be points in the other direction. The Zafimaniry, like other Malagasy, have a word for 'living', *velona*, that applies to all living kinds, as well as to certain stones (for example quartz), clouds, motor engines and so forth, without any indication that these are metaphorical uses. The word for 'dead', *maty*, is even more promiscuous, since it can apply to almost anything that does not work or is broken. To make matters even more complicated, another form of the same root, *faty* (literally 'that which has died', or 'corpse') only applies to humans and a few animals. Thus, a tree can be *maty,* but what remains of it is not its *faty.* Other key words, such as those for 'bearing progeny' or 'being sick', are used for plants as well as for humans and animals; but such usage seems meta-phorical, in that several informants with whom I discussed the matter explicitly said that in spite of common usage rice, for example, 'does not *really* have children'. Thus, the tentative evidence that the examination of the lexicon provides is best understood as meaning that animals are the 'best examples' of being *alive*, while other beings, such as humans, plants and, perhaps, kinds 'we' would consider as definitely not alive, such as clouds, are less typical, and things like mushrooms are on the far periphery of the life prototype.[5] Not only does this seem to me the situation for the Zafimaniry but, on purely anecdotal evidence, it seems also to be the case for many other cultures, including European ones. And it is, of course, also the case described by a number of psychologists for very young American children. I wonder, however, whether in contexts less formal than experimental situations, such a lack of sharp boundary and clarity would not still be implicitly present in the knowledge of adults (Descola 1996). It is because of such ethnographic observations that the psychological theories of Atran and Keil seem ultimately to be unsatisfactory.

The rival, but related, theories of another psychologist, Susan Carey, somewhat modified for anthropological purposes, seem much more appropriate to the data. In addition, they enable us to advance in our understanding of the *content* of the concept of life. Carey's starting point is similar to that of Atran and Keil. It is the general cognitive theory of domain-specificity, as set out most recently by Sperber (1994). The most telling reason for positing that the entire human nervous system is modular and that it is innately differentiated into discrete domains for the understanding of specific kinds of data is the speed with which children learn about these phenomena. Chomsky convincingly argues that children could not possibly learn natural language as fast as they do without being biologically predisposed for it; this explains the fact that all natural languages share a common deep structure. There must therefore be, according to him, a different domain for language, ready-made for this use, and quite different from other mental capacities. In a similar fashion, Sperber and Atran argue that the speed with which children learn about living kinds, and the cross-cultural universality of this knowledge, suggest the existence of an innate disposition for understanding this kind of thing in a special way that is organized differently from other types of knowledge.

Carey agrees that the speed of learning and the universality of the knowledge about living kinds suggest an element of innate predisposition and domain-specificity, but she differs from the writers discussed above in that she rejects the evidence for an innate domain for folk biology as such. Instead, and basing herself on considerable experimental work, she argues that the construction of a living-kind domain in children is a gradual and entirely learned phenomenon, made possible by another, better documented and, in this case, probably innate domain, labelled variously by different writers as the 'folk psychology domain', the 'naive psychology domain', the 'theory of mind domain', or the 'meta-representational domain' (Sperber 1994 and 1996). The naive psychology involved in such a domain is the ability to interpret animation as the sign of intentionality, or, in other words, the imaginative attribution of a mind to other beings. Such an ability enables very young children, as young as two hours old, to distinguish between self-motivated and non-self-motivated phenomena, and to behave quite differently to those to which a 'mind' is attributed. This faculty lies at the very basis of all forms of communication, especially with other humans (Premack and Premack 1994). For Carey, it is the gradual development of such an innate ability that leads to the later construction of the living-kind domain (Carey 1985 and 1996).

The process of this construction according to Carey is roughly as follows. At first, the attribution of a 'mind' to animate, and only animate, objects is very uncertain, leading to the kind of phenomena that Piaget labels 'childhood animism'. Later, this attribution gets anchored to humans and animals and, in an uncertain way, gets transformed into a 'theory of life'. This too is, at first, uncertain, and Carey stresses the difficulty young children have in grasping the meaning of, for example, death. Are statues dead in the same way as grandfathers are?... The child is not too sure. Later on, such things get fairly thoroughly sorted out, as does the distinction between humans and other animals, but, at first, this too is not entirely clear. Then, later, perhaps as late as ten, the notion of 'living things' gets expanded from animals to people, and so as to include plants, and presumably trees, so that, in the end, the adult idea of 'life' is fully formulated.

Carey is particularly interesting for anthropologists because such a developmental process actually turns our attention to the *content* of the cognition of 'life'. First, she stresses the recognition of intentionality in other animate beings as its *fons et origo*, thereby ensuring a permanently peripheral position to plants. Secondly, she studies the inductions made by children about what it is to be alive. For example, if children are told rabbits have an organ with an invented name, will they also believe that cats, humans, daisies and motor cars also have such an organ? The result of this work demonstrates that even adults hold a graded notion of life – i.e. that objects are 'more or less alive'. This graded view is particularly clear in the case of children, though with growing maturity the type of inductions made by Carey's subjects come to resemble more the scientific view, though never becoming identical with it. This means that people's notion of 'life' is much more ragged and provisional than we would imagine from the writings of, for example, Atran.

The significance of such a finding, and the reason why it is so attractive to fieldworking anthropologists, is that, although Carey's work is concerned with American children and adults, anecdotal evidence suggests that it corresponds well with what we find in other societies, and therefore it makes ethnographic observations, such as those described above for the Zafimaniry, much more comprehensible and likely. The value of such a position is not only that it gives real insight into the content of what is understood by the concept of being alive; it also explains the much more tentative and graded picture we find in the kind of ethnographic data most anthropologists have recorded.

There is a difficulty in Carey's argument. American children after the age of ten have constructed a hard and fast 'living kind domain' capable of sustaining exactly the same intuitions that Atran or Sperber consider universal and innate, while Zafimaniry adults are tentative in this matter in a way that seems to resemble the approach of American seven-year-olds. We should be wary, however, in arguing from this that Zafimaniry adults are like American children. Rather, it is quite obvious to me that, in matters biological, the average Zafimaniry, with her or his closer involvement with the forest and agriculture, is far more knowledgeable than the average American.

However, there might be another interpretation of Carey's – and others' – findings regarding the systematicity of biological knowledge in older American children than one couched merely in term of cognitive development. By the age of ten, and perhaps sometimes even seven, American children are thoroughly formally schooled in biology. And since the test situation in Carey's experiments must be very reminiscent for those who undergo it of the formal education with which they are familiar, it would not be surprising that they should respond in such situations as they would in school, and therefore produce a quasi-scientific version of their understanding of 'life'. This would in no way exclude their retaining, in informal and practical contexts at least, a conceptualization that reflects more closely the tentative process by which a living-kind domain has been established for them. This sort of situation has, indeed, been shown to exist for the understanding of physics among American college students. It seems therefore quite possible that the tentative and gradual process uncovered by Carey continues to characterize adult American knowledge in less formal contexts.

This hypothesis is supported by the fact that most Westerners, including Americans, can sympathize with and even assent to such 'unscientific' statements as 'plants are less alive than butterflies', even though they have been taught to *know* better. If this is so, Westerners would, in informal contexts, be very similar to the Zafimaniry, and the developmental story told by Carey would underlie many of the nuances, subtleties and uncertainties that we find in the ethnographic data and in the informal intuitions of everyone.

In particular, it would explain the peripheral 'living kind' status of plants in general, and that of trees in particular, in all cultures. This is due to the fact that plants are apparently inanimate, and that it is therefore difficult, or paradoxical, to attribute intentionality to them, while this attribution of intentionality remains, for everyone, the core theory of the concept of 'life'. Understood in this way, Carey's work concords well with the ethnographic data discussed above and, for that matter, with such observations as the fact that Western animal rights protesters are more concerned with cruelty toward sheep than toward spiders, and very rarely feel strongly about the killing of moulds. In fact, such a graded picture of life does more; it suggests a possible explanation of the symbolical uses of plants and trees.

THE SYMBOLICAL FUNCTIONS OF PLANTS AND TREES

The starting point of this chapter was the observation that symbolism used in ritual is to be understood in terms of conceptual analogies, which are based on perceived continuities and discontinuities, and that, in the case of living kinds, the continuity we find most often stressed is the presence of life, while the discontinuities may be such things as the inability to speak, promiscuous sexuality, or differences in lifespans. In rituals, these continuities and discontinuities are exploited as avenues for establishing connections and operating disconnections. This is because rituals have a purpose: to cure, for example. This purpose is achieved by connecting related entities, which therefore must have an apparently 'real' and convincing unity between them, e.g. animals and people, and then disconnecting them, because of their 'real' and convincing difference. During the disconnection (for example, killing), transformations are carried out or recognized in the symbol that cannot be carried out on the principal entity. Then, the original connection is re-established once again because of its 'real' and convincing character, so that those for whom the ritual is carried out can benefit from the results of the operations carried out on the symbolic entity. This is done by demonstrating their apparent unity. Ritual practices depend, therefore, on the complex demonstrable 'real' and convincing proximity, and on the 'real' and convincing distance of the symbols and the subjects of the ritual. They must be neither too close nor too distant and, in fact, the more ambiguous, yet convincing, the relationship, the more it can be evoked and used in this game of 'one moment I am here, the next I am not'. Animals that are clearly alive, but not human, serve well in this game, in which the ambiguities are played out around their problematic intentionality. Thus, not surprisingly, it is precisely upon the problem of the attribution of intentionality to beings more or less distant from humans, imaginary or not, who are more or less 'alive', that so much of religion hinges (Boyer 1994; Sperber 1994).

The same sort of games can be played with plants, where, again, the difficult relation of the presence and absence of intentionality and life is stressed. In the case of trees, a further element can be introduced: games around the issue of the presence of life itself, because of the uncertainty of whether plants and trees are fully alive or not. This is certainly the motor of Zafimaniry symbolism, and it depends on the fact that, for them, being alive is not a clear-cut matter as would be implied if we followed Atran, but is, in the case of trees, a questionable *theory*, as Carey suggests it is for children, and as I argue it probably is also for all adults.

Psychological theories such as Carey's are of relevance, therefore, for the discussion of recurrences in the nature of religious symbolism, because these studies concern the cognitive bases out of which such symbolism is built. They can explain the opportunities that such cognition offers for religious constructions (as does here the 'more or less' character of the conceptualization of life) and, to a certain extent, account for them. If, as in this case, there is a good reason to believe that the type of cognition in question is not culturally variable, we then have the added benefit that such studies inevitably suggest a credible explanation for the regularities in the symbolism we find in different cultures. It is the universality in the conceptualization of 'life' that explains the universal aspects of plant and tree symbolism, the presence of which will strike the reader of this book as he or she reads about so many specific cases. However, drawing attention to this cognitive anchoring does not, and cannot, fully account for the phenomena themselves. If it pretended to do so, it would ignore the very great element of variation that is also just as present as the regularities. But, in fact, this is no real problem for the theoretical position adopted here, which can accommodate variation as well as recurrence. First of all, the cognitive anchor proposed is itself a shifting anchor, since it consists, not of a simple categorical 'theory of life', but of a 'theory of life' that applies differentially and contextually to different types of beings. Secondly, it is essential for understanding the theoretical thrust of the argument to remember that it can only be *one* explanatory element 'awaiting' to be combined with ecological and historical explanations before a fuller account of particular ethnographic cases can be given, even if, in practice, this remains an impossible goal.

NOTES

1. A difference that the Zafimaniry elaborate further by finding finer discriminations between the lifespans of different tree species, and using them analogically to compare and comment on different types of people.
2. For a discussion of whether this is legitimate, see *inter alia* Atran 1990: 67.
3. Often forgetting about non-living natural kinds.
4. See the footnote to Carey 1996: 275.
5. Such an assertion is anecdotal, inasmuch as all anthropological statements of this sort are; they would merit more systematic study.

REFERENCES

Arhem, K. 1996. 'The Cosmic Food Web: Human–nature Relatedness in the Northwest Amazon', in P. Descola and G. Palsson (eds), *Nature and Society*, London: Routledge.

Atran, S. 1990. *Cognitive Foundations of Natural History*, Cambridge: Cambridge University Press.

Berlin, B., J. Breedlove and P. Raven. 1973. 'General Principles and Nomenclature in Folk Biology', *American Anthropologist* 75: 214–42.

Bloch, M. 1992a. *Prey into Hunter: The Politics of Religious Experience*, Cambridge: Cambridge University Press.

—— 1992b. 'What Goes Without Saying: the Conceptualization of Zafimaniry Society', in A. Kuper (ed.), *Conceptualizing Society*, London: Routledge.

—— 1993 'Domain Specificity, Living Kinds and Symbolism', in P. Boyer (ed.), *Cognitive Aspects of Religious Symbolism*, Cambridge: Cambridge University Press.

Boyer, P. 1994. *The Naturalness of Religious Ideas*, Cambridge: Cambridge University Press.

Carey, S. 1985. *Conceptual Change in Childhood*, Cambridge, MA: MIT Press.

—— 1996. 'On the Origin of Causal Understanding', in S. Carey and D. Sperber (eds), *Causal Understanding*, Cambridge: Cambridge University Press.

Dahl, G. and A. Hjort. 1976. *Having Herds: Pastoral Herd Growth and Household Economy*, Stockholm: University of Stockholm.

Descola, P. 1992. 'Societies of Nature, and the Nature of Society', in A. Kuper (ed.), *Conceptualizing Society*, London: Routledge.

—— 1996. 'Constructing Natures: Symbolic Ecology and Social Practice', in P. Descola and G. Palsson (eds), *Nature and Society*, London: Routledge.

Ellen, R. 1996. 'The Cognitive Geometry of Nature: a Contextual Approach', in P. Descola and G. Palsson (eds), *Nature and Society*, London: Routledge.

Fortes, M. 1972. 'Totem and Taboo', *Proceedings of the Royal Anthropological Institute for 1966*.

Karim, W.-J. 1981. *Ma'Bedisek Concepts of Living Things*, London: Athlone.

Keil, F. 1992. *Concepts, Kinds, and Cognitive Development*, Cambridge, MA: MIT Press.

Lakoff, G. 1987. *Women, Fire and Dangerous Things*, Chicago: Chicago University Press.

Lévi-Strauss, C. 1962. *La Pensée sauvage*, Paris: Plon.

Premack, D. and A. Premack. 1994. 'Moral Belief: Form versus Content', in L. Hirschfeld and S. Gelman (eds), *Mapping the Mind*, Cambridge: Cambridge University Press.

Rappaport, R. 1968. *Pigs for the Ancestors*, New Haven: Yale University Press.

Rival, L. 1996. 'Blowpipes and Spears: the Social Significance of Huaorani Technological Choices', in P. Descola and G. Palsson (eds), *Nature and Society*, London: Routledge.

Sperber, D. 1994. 'The Modularity of Thought and the Epidemiology of Representations', in L. Hirschfeld and S. Gelman (eds), *Mapping the Mind*, Cambridge: Cambridge University Press.

—— 1996. *La Contagion des idées: théorie naturaliste de la culture*, Paris: Odile Jacob.

Tambiah, S. 1969. 'Animals are Good to Think and to Prohibit', *Ethnology* 8: 423–59.

Turner, V. 1968. *The Forest of Symbols: Aspects of Ndembu Ritual*, Ithaca: Cornell University Press.

CHAPTER 3

QUESTIONS NOT TO ASK OF MALAGASY CARVINGS

Maurice Bloch

This chapter is a cautionary tale or a short history of the attempts at interpretation of the carvings of a group of people in Madagascar: the Zafimaniry.

The Zafimaniry are swidden cultivators living in the eastern forest of Madagascar and they number about 40,000. However, they are famous because they are one of the few groups which originally produced the kind of things museums and tourists can take away and display, and subsequently they have developed a tourist-goods industry of some significance. Here I am concerned with their traditional carvings. These are low reliefs or engravings of relatively elaborate geometrical patterns which cover the wooden parts of their houses – especially the shutters and, most beautifully, the three main posts. Since the 1920s, at least, professional and amateur anthropologists and archaeologists have bothered the Zafimaniry by asking them what these carvings 'meant'. Included among these, in the recent past, has been myself.

I say what these carvings 'meant', but this is a tricky word indeed. What I am talking about is in part the trickiness of the word. There is of course a massive, almost infinite literature in philosophy and linguistics on the topic, but here I simply want to consider the problems of the word when applied to this type of material culture and then in a rather matter-of-fact way, since this is one of the kind of cases which anthropologists and archaeologists deal with.

The people who interrogated various Zafimaniry and then went on to write articles or books in order to report the answers they were given did

Figure 3.1 Malagasy carvings

not use the word 'meant', because they were writing in French. This is
not quite such a trivial point as it might seem, because already in French
there is no equivalent to the English verb 'to mean'. One can ask the
'sense' (which perhaps corresponds to the English meaning) or one can
use the phrase (and that is the phrase used by the writers) *vouloir dire,*
'try to say'. These authors tell us, then, what these carvings are 'trying to

say'. If there is a problem between French and English, it is not surprising that there is also one between French and Malagasy. All the writers concerned purport to report Zafimaniry answers to their question – but to what question? First of all, the authors fall into two categories. Two of them can speak Malagasy, in both cases probably better than I can (one of them is a native speaker); the others must have used an interpreter who was presumably landed with the critical task of rendering into Malagasy the French phrase *vouloir dire*. How did they do it? I can only guess from my attempts to ask the same thing in Malagasy. One can ask something which is a bit like the English 'What is the point of', a phrase which is the rare positive of a commonly used catchphrase which means 'there is no point to it' *(antony);* or one can use a rather ontological phrase which asks, 'What is the root cause of this?' *(fototry);* or one can ask for the engravings, 'What are those pictures of?'; or you can ask people as they are doing the carvings, 'What are you doing?' None of these questions really conveys what either the French or the English terms convey. In any case, when I asked these questions of the Zafimaniry during my first fieldwork there I obtained rather disappointing answers. To the question 'What are those pictures of?' I was answered with great certainty that they were pictures of nothing. When I asked for a cause or the point of the carvings I triggered the ready-made phrase that there was no point, and when I asked what people were doing I was told 'Carving'. There was actually one answer I was given very often, but I felt it was so bland and therefore frustrating that I paid no attention to it and did not even put it down in my field notes. It was that 'It made the wood beautiful'.

I want to return to this in a moment; but first, a word about what the other writers say they were told. Apparently they did not have the same frustrating experience as I did – or, at least, give no hints of this. My first reaction to their apparent success, when I knew perfectly well that all these people had merely been passing through, when I had spent a considerable time with the Zafimaniry and spoke their language, was that these authors were mainly making it up. Now I am a little more charitable – at least, in the case of two of them, one of whom is the native speaker I referred to above. I don't think these two were lying – simply that they were misleading. These authors report that various parts of the carvings are representational; that, for example, the ubiquitous circular designs represent the moon and that some of the designs, which appear like shading, are rain.

I think I now know what they are talking about. As a result of subsequent fieldwork I was told by certain expert carvers somewhat similar things about various designs commonly used by the Zafimaniry. However, in following these up it was made very clear that what was meant was that these were 'the names' of these designs. It is not that they represent the phenomena but that the names indicate a trivial similarity which can be used as an indicator of the design when, for example, you ask a carver to do a particular design for your house. It is rather like herringbone tweed. Clearly the tweed is not a picture of the osature of the fish.

All this, however, does not mean that I have nothing to say about these carvings, and I shall try to explain how I feel able to move on. This is partly as a result of the fact that someone once elaborated the remark that the carvings make the wood beautiful by adding 'They honour the wood'. Immediately I realized that the bland statement was not so bland after all since its focus was not beautification in general but beautification of the wood. But really this was only a hint. In fact the only useful answer the Zafimaniry could have given me and the other researchers to our questions was the famous one: 'If I were you, mate, I would not be starting from here.'

Where one needs to start is with an understanding of the significance of houses and the wood the carvings decorate, and I briefly shall try to indicate this.

For the Zafimaniry, houses are the basis of ordered society and the mark of a successful life; this is because they are the outward side of a successful marriage. For the Zafimaniry, going through life successfully is a gradual process of settling down, of which marriage is an essential element, and growth through the production of children, grandchildren, etc., who are the continuation of the couple. When children are young they are undetermined in place, substance or morality. Their bodies are malleable so that they are permanently affected by their environment. They don't have a home of their own. They don't take part in agriculture, but they hunt and gather all over the place, they play in a chaotic way, their language is not well rounded. The attachments they form – and these include sexual attachments very early on – are chaotic and impermanent. But then, gradually, they settle spatially, physically and psychologically as they move toward marriage – and marriage takes material form in the house they begin to build and furnish. The young man will put up the central house-posts and a flimsy outer wall of reeds and mats, the young woman will bring the furniture of the hearth. This building is the flimsy beginning of marriage; but if the relationship settles down (which may or may not happen) – above all, if the couple start to produce children – the house will harden. That is, the flimsy materials will, little by little over many years, begin to be replaced by massive vertical pieces of wood. It is as if the body of the pair as individuals begins to fade in significance and instead it is replaced by the building of their mutuality. This is expressed in a number of ways but, above all, by the oft-stressed observation that the house is acquiring bones: that is, the pieces of wood. And the wood that is used is not any wood; it is wood from the hardest, longest-lasting trees, and it is not any part of the tree, but the hardest impacted heartwood of these woods which the Zafimaniry call by a word which literally means 'to last'. The aesthetic and moral value of the hardness of such wood, especially the fact that it is a hardness produced from an original softness (the young plant), totally dominates Zafimaniry discourse in a way which would almost be impossible to overemphasize. This house and this wood can be seen as material culture, but to an extent this is misleading in that such a phrase suggests something different from non-material culture. It would be quite misleading to see Zafimaniry houses as expressing Zafimaniry marriage and society or containing married pairs. The house is the marriage. With time, the original couple (in human form) will die and the children, grandchildren, great-grandchildren will disperse, but ideally neither of these processes will occur completely. This is because these descendants will gather on occasion in the house to settle disputes or ask blessings from the original couple – or, rather, from the house or parts of that house such as the cooking pot and posts. The original couple therefore survives and continues to grow as their progeny multiply – and so will the house. The descendants soon take over the business of the house, at first during the life of the original couple and then without interruption after their death. The house will continue to harden and become more and more bony. This is a process which is never complete, partly because some wood will need replacing but also because the hardening is in fact endless. Even if the wood of the house is very hard and sound there is a continuation to the process of hardening and transformation, and that continuation is carving. Carving 'honours' the hardness of the heartwood and makes it even more evident and beautiful.

The carvings are therefore the continuation of the process of human maturation and settling down, of marriage and house creation, of hardening, of growth, of acquiring bones. The carvings are not separate from this process, they are not representing, they are part of the finishing of a task which should never finish as it should grow for ever. The carvings are a celebration of the material and the building and of a successful life which continues to expand and reproduce (and, by the way, this is why the carvings must remain shallow engravings because otherwise they would be negating their very purpose by weakening the wood).

The carvings are not pointing outwards – mutely trying to say something, *voulant dire* as the questions expected – they are an essential element of the material and the social principle on which they occur; they are not referring or signifying. The beautifying is merely the extension of the making and being of the wood and the house and growth of the original marriage. The carvings are the continuation and magnification (as in *magnificat)* of the growth and success of the couple transcending the impermanence of life.

CHAPTER 4

COMMENSALITY AND POISONING

Maurice Bloch

In all societies, sharing food is a way of establishing closeness, while, conversely, the refusal to share is one of the clearest marks of distance and enmity. These points have been repeatedly made by both anthropologists and psychologists (Miller, Fiske and Rozin 1998). Commensality, the action of eating together, is thus one of the most powerful operators of the social process.

The reason is that the sharing of food is, and is always seen to be, in some way or other, the sharing of that which will cause, or at least maintain, a common substance among those who commune together. I use the word 'commune' here to evoke the Christian communion, the commemoration of the Last Supper, itself a transformation of the Jewish Passover feast (Feeley-Harnik 1981). These are rituals that can be associated with that loose class of ceremonies that go under the label of 'sacrifice', a most characteristic feature of which is the triumphal closing communal meal, usually of meat. This commensual aspect of sacrifice is an old theme in anthropology, first fully developed by the nineteenth-century theologian Robertson-Smith, but which I, among others, have also recently discussed (Bloch 1992a). However, the image of eating together as a form of communion is also found in much less complex and elevated practices such as the daily domestic meal of families across the globe, or even, and equally intriguingly, if less openly, in the flirtatious practice of eating out of each other's plates, common in French restaurants and elsewhere.[1]

If the theme of eating in common is universally an indication and a creator of bodily propinquity, this does not mean that we should forget the great differences that exist between cultures. This kind of semi-universal phenomenon (I use the contradiction in the terms advisedly) is an example of a familiar and awkward problem that continually has dogged the whole history of anthropology. First, we notice very obvious similarities across cultures that tempt us too quickly forward, toward grand generalizations that are then followed by the realization that there are differences, a setback that makes us retreat so completely that we seem to have nothing to say and that we deny the very reality that encouraged us in the first place. This is the difficulty of these loosely similar points of departure of which the meanings evoked by commensality are typical and which probably will have, in the end, to be explained by theories other than the familiar comparative method of anthropology. Here, therefore, I limit myself to evoking one of the 'almost recurrent' meanings of commensality by exploring briefly ethnographic examples, some of which I know from first hand and others for which I will rely on the literature. Only then will I venture a little further and begin to attempt to try to account for these incomplete regularities.

In considering any particular instance of the social significance of the sharing, or not, of food, anthropologists have usually paid particular attention to three factors. These are: (1) the symbolic significance of different foods; (2) the symbolic significance of different ways of preparing food; and (3) the relation of ideas concerning sharing substance through food and through procreation and sex. I shall take these three topics in turn before considering a particular example from Madagascar, where we shall see the three factors working together. Finally, this example will lead me to a consideration of some of the less attractive aspects of food sharing, for example the disgust it may cause and even its association with antisocial behaviour.

THE DIFFERENTIAL SIGNIFICANCE OF SHARING DIFFERENT TYPES OF FOOD

There are similarities attributed to the significance of sharing particular foods across cultures but the differences, nonetheless, are wide. Thus, sharing wild honey in some African societies may be a powerful declaration of male solidarity, whereas it can be simply neutral, for example, in highland Philippines. However, it is the significance of sharing different foods within the same culture that has proved a particularly fruitful line of enquiry in anthropology. In particular, given the focus of this chapter, it is interesting to note how particular groups of people may view some foods as better social *conductors* than others: in France, for example, the eating of soup together implies a greater degree of togetherness than does eating popcorn. This example also shows that there is usually not a single scale of social conductivity in a single cultural context but several. The sharing of soup here is, to borrow from Durkheim, a sign of strong familial *organic* solidarity among people who are joined by their dissimilarity, whereas the sharing of popcorn is, to a certain extent, a sign of an egalitarian mechanical solidarity of a different sort. In this case, therefore, we find two co-occurring but different registers within which social conductivity is evaluated, whereas these evaluations are difficult to calibrate across registers.

The rankings and registers of social conductivity, just alluded to, often resemble each other across cultures, but these resemblances are, unfortunately, yet another case of the curse of the 'semi-universality' mentioned above, which therefore tempts us to generalize further than caution would advise. In a general discussion such as this, however, I hope that such recklessness may be forgiven and viewed as, above all, a stimulus toward further research. So we may note in passing that in many, often quite unrelated, cultures the sharing of meat is a sign of a supreme closeness, though of a closeness that is usually understood as exceptional and which makes meat eating particularly suitable for feasts and celebrations. This may have something to do with the physiological kick that fat gives in diets where it is lacking; it may also be because animal flesh recalls the human flesh that it will contribute to create – a parallelism that further may evoke representations of an exchange of death for life. This particular symbolism is often explicitly alluded to in rituals of the sacrificial kind. In this type of ceremony we often find a preference for the meat of large animals whose slaughter is spectacular. Conversely, the parallel between the two kinds of flesh also causes the near universal unease surrounding the slaughter of large animals in places where this has become a secular everyday occurrence (Vialles 1994) or even where it is a rarer occasion (Hugh-Jones 1996).

It would be wrong, however, to imagine that it is only meat that is considered as the supreme conductor of social identity. In a somewhat different way, this role is often given over to rice in Asian cultures. The link between the body of the consumers and this food is perhaps nowhere expressed better than among the Iban of Borneo, where each family used a genetically distinct strain of rice for food and for seed and normally avoided all others. In this way, the Iban could imagine their society in terms of a naturalized permanence where a particular genetic line of people was linked forever with a particular genetic line of grain. This has further implications. Thus the incorporation through marriage of a new spouse, an introduction of foreign genetic material that will strengthen the line, can also be represented and thought of in terms of food: the newcomer is brought in by means of his/her ritual ingestion of the rice of the family he or she is about to join (Freeman 1958). The closeness of rice and humans can manifest itself in many other ways in Southeast Asia. Thus, Trankell describes how, in northern Thailand, the particularly lengthy process of preparing sticky rice, with its double cooking, is strongly valued, precisely because of its laboriousness and difficulty. The sequence of actions required is seen as that which animates, in all senses of the word, the very being of a united family (Trankell 1995).

THE PROCESSING OF FOOD

Lévi-Strauss is one anthropologist who has stressed the differential social significance of different types of food preparation. He draws our attention to the different and contrasting evocations – often attributed to boiled and roasted foods, as well as the stronger contrasts of cooked food with foods whose preparation requires some form of rotting, such as cheese, or foods eaten raw and unprepared (Lévi-Strauss 1968). Perhaps nothing illustrates better the different conductivity of these different modes of preparation than the case of traditional India. There high-caste individuals would refuse boiled rice from a low-caste person, but would accept fried rice because the heat of the process had, somehow, made the food a less potent and thus less dangerous communicator of ritual pollution. Much more complex distinctions are often made both in India and beyond. In much of Southeast Asia, meals require boiled foods, and if this is present it implies a form of total social commitment that inevitably suggests kinship. On the other hand, what we can call snacks, not because they are not elaborate or plentiful but because they do not comprise boiled food, become suitable for the lesser social commitment of gatherings of non-kin such as, for example, the members of savings associations.

FOOD AND KINSHIP

This last contrast, between the food of associations based merely on a practical purpose and the food of the family, brings me to the most thought-provoking and perhaps the most complex aspect of the potential significance of commensality. Since the sharing of food expresses, and is also believed to cause, the bodily unification of the persons who eat together, it represents something similar to ideas about the unity between parents and children that is understood to result from the processes of procreation, or to the bodily unification that may be imagined to result from sexual intercourse.[2]

The kinds of substantial unity evoked by food and kinship are, therefore, often in a dialectic relationship. Both are involved in the multistranded process of joining and rejoining that which was and would become separate.

In the case of kinship, in the common representations of human biology found in different cultures, the child is at first conceptualized as being one body with its mother, perhaps also with its father, but as gradually becoming with time more and more separated from its parents. This temporal separation also implies that siblings will grow apart as they become older. In a similar way, sexual partners that previously were separate bodies become united and may be believed to exchange something and therefore substantially unify, though this unification through sex is at the same time a further factor in the separation of those who were once united by birth and siblingship. This separation being the inevitable result of the incest taboo requires that sexual unification be with relative strangers. The flow of life implied by kinship and marriage is therefore perceived as a matter of bodies uniting and separating and uniting again.

Commensality evokes a similar dialectical process of temporal unification and diversification. Eating the same food unites the bodies that eat together and eating different foods distances them. This is particularly so when commensality involves eating 'good conductor' foods, prepared by highly conductive techniques. As a result, families may be understood as being continually unified not only by biology but also by being commensal units. Thus, in a recent study, the French sociologist Anne Muxel shows that it is in terms of the recalling of shared meals that individuals' memory of their family is realized (Muxel 1996). But then, as people grow older, if they are to participate in a wider social process, they will come to share the food of strangers; thus, as with sex, this exogamic commensality, because it joins bodies, will also relatively separate those who were previously united. As in the light of kinship, so in the light of food, life is understood as a continual process of bodily mergings and divisions.

A good example of this dual process is provided by Carsten in her discussion of Malay culture (Carsten 1997). There, the sharing of food is seen as establishing a bodily link almost as strong as the sharing of the substance that comes about in sexual union or the passing on of substance that occurs in childbirth. Indeed, the process of the maturation of the child in the womb is explicitly paralleled with the transformation of food from a foreign raw substance into something that will sustain and therefore continue the family through time. Thus, among Malays, being one family, one kinship group, one local group cannot be envisaged in terms that do not, in part, refer to the act of eating that which has been cooked on one hearth, whereas eating with strangers implies a separation of the original familial unity.

As a result, as in this case, the concepts of kinship and commensality act together and are often believed to imply one another. Breastfeeding is often seen as the natural continuation of the linkage of the body of mother and child to the extent that, as in the Arab world, rules of incest often apply to people who, though unrelated by kinship, have been breastfed by the same woman.

In fact, in all cases, kinship created through birth is believed to be less negotiable and therefore less potentially innovative than the unification coming from food and sex. These are therefore often seen as tools in the hands of actors by which they can affect, change, or tune the unnegotiable aspect of parenthood and siblingship.

A MALAGASY EXAMPLE

The way these different factors come together can be illustrated by a single example. For this, I turn to my long-term fieldwork among a group of people in Madagascar, the Zafimaniry. These form a group who were traditionally slash and burn cultivators, growing maize, beans, etc., but who are now increasingly turning to irrigated rice because of deforestation. They number around 40,000 and live in the east-coast forest of the great Island.

There is a lot to be said about their kinship system; but it can also be described, and this is what they do themselves, as though it was extraordinarily simple. This is done in terms of a dominant image – of one well-maintained house inhabited by a single nuclear family. The family is thus visualized largely in terms of the building and the location where the building is situated; it is thus a group gathered around the central post of the house, eating food cooked from the house's single hearth (Bloch 1992b). The kinship terms used for address and description among the people are few[3] and easily glossed into English as 'father', 'mother', 'child', 'older sibling', 'younger sibling'.

It might at first be thought that these few terms would be insufficient to denote more remote relatives who do not live inside the one house. This is not so, because these terms can also be used for relatives who, in English, would be considered more remote: first cousins, for example, are referred to by the term for siblings, and this would in theory also be true for any cousin of one's own generation, however remote. The same is the case at the parental level, where any related adult of one's parent's generation is called by the terms used for one's own parents. Again, the same principle applies for the generation below. Part of the explanation for this apparently promiscuous extension of familial terms lies again in the fact that representations of kinship are dominated by the image of the single house with its elementary family. When the elementary terms are used to describe or address relatives who do not actually live in one house, these terms nonetheless evoke, through an implicit allusion, a single household: this is the house and the nuclear parental household of earlier generations, for example common grandparents, or, as the case requires, much more ancient ascendants and their houses, people who will most probably have disappeared long ago, although their houses may still be standing and be the object of an ancestral cult. This means that, in terms of a great-grandparental household, second cousins can be seen as 'co-children' of the adults of this evoked house, if, as is the case for the Zafimaniry, the term 'child' can mean both 'children' and 'children's offspring'. From the perspective of this evoked, but disappeared, nuclear family and their house, second cousins *are* siblings. As a result, since the population of the Zafimaniry is not large and the number of people interacting is limited, everybody can be, and should be, treated in this domestic idiom, because it is always possible to evoke a house in which the people with whom one is interacting are 'co-children' with oneself.

Of course, not everybody is thought of as equally close, and some people are clearly experienced as more remote, perhaps because of genealogical distance, perhaps because of geographical distance, or simply because one does not like them much. In such cases, although it would be offensive in the extreme not to refer to them as 'brothers', 'sisters', 'mothers', 'fathers' or 'children' to their face, as soon as they have turned their back, people are quick to explain to strangers, who might really think that, for example, the visitor from a remote village one was just talking to was actually a full sister of one's companion, that, really, this person was called 'sister' *only* because the two share great-great-grandparents, or whatever the case may be.[4]

By means of the device of the evocation of past houses and households, the dominant theme of Zafimaniry kinship is that it is simply a matter of elementary families living in one house. This image encompasses the central role given to commensality because one of the most important aspects of the prototypical house/family scene is a communal meal of food cooked on a single hearth by the 'mother'. In this evocation, this commensal meal entails kinship *and* shared bodily substance; in such a situation whether it is commensality that creates kinship or kinship that creates commensality is a question totally obscured by this holistic representation. However, this *evidence,* as we shall see, hides the same ambiguities that lie behind the apparently simple system suggested by the kinship terms.[5]

This is because, in exactly the same way as remote kin (and that includes all Zafimaniry) are treated terminologically as though they were part of one's own elementary family by evoking a household scene in a house that has probably disappeared long ago, so too, in terms of food, these 'relatives' must be treated as though they truly belonged to the house they are, in fact, probably merely visiting. This means that any stranger to the domestic unit will always be invited to come and partake of meals with phrases such as 'come and eat, my child' or 'my mother', 'my father', 'my older sibling', 'my younger sibling', and under normal circumstances it is impossible to refuse such an invitation. Hence, the circle of commensuals is also stereotypically anchored in the image of the elementary family, but in fact it is always potentially expandable to everybody and anybody with whom one comes into contact. This potential is commonly realized as, without warning, the commensual family circle is expanded to include people of different degrees of closeness who are treated, outwardly at least, as 'one of the family'.

The same logic operates on a grand scale in feasts. These bring together large groups of people who, it is presumed and always emphatically stated, are the *children* of one household or other, which existed in the past, but which unfortunately has become divided by the passage of generations and the intrusion of marriage links. In the feast, however, these children are gathered together, eating together: they are one once again. Such a statement of oneness is, however, at one level, also well understood as a denial of the reality of life outside the festive context, because everybody knows that, when those present go home, they will then belong to different, perhaps competing, households. The context of the feast thus brings back the contradiction that is highlighted when those who, at one moment, call a person a true sibling and afterwards say she is no such thing. However, to see in all this simply a mere polite white lie would be too simple, as it would be to ignore the full meaning of commensality.

This is because we must not forget that eating together is not a mere reflection of common substance, it is also a mechanism that creates it. As noted above, normally the consubstantiation that comes from kinship and commensality are so tightly bound that they cannot be thought of separately; but when they become separated we can see that they operate differently and even that a dialectic exists between them.

Before exploring this, however, it is necessary to understand the significance of the food itself for the Zafimaniry. The basic meal, which for them carries all the symbolic weight of communion, consists of a combination of a staple, usually dried maize and a few beans, and a tiny relish that can be almost any type of vegetable, fish, or more occasionally meat. Nothing is comparable with this type of meal in terms of significance. Apart from the foods that are included in such a meal, there are, however, also foods and combinations of food that are less meaningful. The foods that are accorded least social import are wild food such as shrimps, small fish, or fruit and berries. I am tempted to say that these have, according to Zafimaniry views, no true nutritive value in that they do not strengthen and build the body, and therefore are not taken seriously. Their lack of significance, however, also indicates that they have no social value in that they do not bind people. The nutritive and social aspects are thus truly inseparable. Roasted foods, whether they be corn cobs or bits of meat, are also not the foods of communion though they often are seen as a kind of promise of the communion of boiled food. Thus at the beginning of feasts, when a large animal has been killed, people eat with great excitement bits of roast liver on skewers, in anticipation of the meal whose preparation through boiling will take a much longer time. Finally, eating boiled food without relish, or relish without boiled food, taken in however great quantities, does not bring the familial unity which alone truly nourishes.

Then, even more than the standard meal, there are some foods that are seen as super-conductors of social consubstantiality, what we can call 'rhetorical conductors'. These are honey and rum. Both, although single uncooked substances, are in some way a super and complete meal that can be prepared quickly. These foods however somehow also suggest less familial and intimate acts of communion. The two are not identical. Honey is something one shares with a respected superior and therefore, although it diminishes distance, it does not, like the family meal, remove hierarchy. Rum, on the other hand, diminishes both distance and hierarchy. In the case of honey and rum, commensality does not just abolish distance between those gathered together, but also between the living and the ancestors who are invited to partake in the food and be there again. After all, it is their house that is being reactivated.

This discussion of the different 'conducting' potential of foods shows that they are active factors in creating closeness or, to be more accurate, in recreating closeness, because they bring back people who have been divided by time. Thus, for the Zafimaniry, the dialectic flow of life is created by a balance between actions that join and rejoin (which include birth, sex *and* commensality) and time that gradually separates.

But the joining or rejoining through sex and food are also problematic. Sex, in the Zafimaniry idiom of dominant endogamy, can be understood as bringing those who were once united together again; but it is also well known that, under this vague evocation of regrouping, it can dangerously bring into the domestic unit total strangers who secretly reject its isolationist tendency or who, for a variety of reasons, want to keep their distance.[6] The same is true of food.

For example, the unity of the living and the dead that is brought about in feasts (Astuti 1994) is not only pious, and even jolly, it also has its horrifying aspect. For the Zafimaniry, the dead, as bodies, are terrifying and polluting and, although in feasts they do not return as corpses but in more mysterious ways, something of the horror of the dead still hangs about them. Secondly, although the ancestors care for their descendants, they do it in such a stern way that one does not really want them around too much. This is because their main way of ensuring proper behaviour from their descendants is by sending disease. As a result, the contact and consubstantiality brought about by the feast is both an occasion of joy at being reunited with the dead, and a very uncomfortable affair.

The other source of discomfort in commensality is the fear of poisoning. The Zafimaniry are as obsessed by the theme of poisoning as they are by the theme of domestic oneness. In reality, for them, the two are different sides of the same coin. Whenever one goes away to a foreign village, it is advisable to take a magical antidote to poisoning. The same is true whenever one goes to a feast. The reason is that when one goes to see more distant relatives one will be drawn into that act of substantial domestic unification that is commensality. Commensality abolishes the separation brought about by time, but this separation also has a positive side, for the individual at least. It is the source of independence from one's parents and one's siblings. It has been brought about by marriage that has given you the individual ability to reproduce. It has given you the opportunity to distance yourself from those with whom you may be in competition.[7] Commensality, therefore, threatens independence and throws you into far too great an intimacy with those with whom you may be in conflict. The whole ambiguity of making one those who are in fact separate becomes dangerous. Perhaps, as in the case of a distant relative invited as a 'child' to a foreign house, the person invited and the host were once 'one house'; but that time is long ago, and many divisions have occurred since then, and other ties incompatible with the original household have been created. As a result, there is always the fear that the closeness that is being created by the direct bodily communication that certain foods establish will simply become a means of getting at you. This is what is expressed by the fear of poisoning. And, as might be expected, the better a food is as a conductor that creates bodily closeness, the better it is as a medium of poison.[8]

The fear of poisoning is always present when strangers are treated as close kin, and it is particularly present at feasts when large groups of people suddenly become 'one house' eating from one hearth. Attending feasts is, therefore, particularly dangerous and so, as noted above, all Zafimaniry take protective medicines against poisoning whenever they attend one. The same danger exists with visiting.

This means that every invitation given and accepted is not only an act of solidarity; it is also always a test. Will you dare to eat with me and become one? This unspoken question lies, I would argue, behind all acts of commensality among the Zafimaniry. It is the negative consequence of the meaning given to the positive act of inclusion into a single house and nuclear family that every invitation to share food implies.

Commensality is thus revealed as a social operator of much greater complexity than it appeared at first. It is not merely a binder of the social system, as kinship created by birth is thought to be; it becomes the means by which the domestic house unit can be adventurously expanded by means of an idiom that seems most unadventurous. And the adventures it allows, like all adventures, both are the means by which one's life can be expanded and are dangerous.

COMMENSALITY AS A TEST

I have used this Zafimaniry example to demonstrate how, even when we are dealing with people very different from contemporary Euro-Americans, very familiar themes reappear. I have used it also to show the negative side of commensality in a particularly explicit case. But I am inevitably drawn to asking the question whether the element of dare and testing that exists in Zafimaniry commensality may not also be seen much nearer home, and indeed may be shown to be an essential and inevitable aspect of commensality.

After all, the flirting couple in the French restaurant I alluded to above may not just want to become closer; they may well be challenging and testing each other, to find out how far the other is willing to engage in greater intimacies. They may lie using the easily innovative consubstantiality suggested by commensality to establish, re-establish or modify much less labile commitments. And as they use this supremely creative tool, which disguises its adventurousness behind a show of reassuring homeliness, they are inevitably running the risks of social innovation. This is a generalization that I believe is worth testing further.

There is also another, even more general, way of considering this same issue. Paul Rozin in his writings points out how it is of the nature of an omnivorous species such as ours to be continually testing out new foods and, in the process, overcoming disgust or other off-putting superficialities. Such testing is clearly of value, as it permits the exploitation of a wide range of sources of nutrition, but it is also full of obvious dangers, not least the risk of poisoning. In a social species such as *Homo sapiens,* this testing takes on a social form because it involves not only individual experience, but also accepting the authority of those whom one can trust about the edibility of certain foods. This means that commensality with them is a form of guarantee of non-poisoning.

However, a successful social career cannot be just a matter of keeping close to those whom one has known from birth; it must also be a reasonably adventurous one, involving the formation of bonds beyond one's immediate family. These new bonds, in order to have some sort of moral guarantee, are likely to have to use the very representations of the more familiar ties that they transcend. In other words, if these new bonds are to have some of the emotional power of the close relationships, the forming of these bonds will involve taking the risk of projecting familial behaviours on to relative strangers. One of these behaviours is commensality, where the risks involved in eating are normally neutralized by eating with those one knows well. If one has to, or wants to, eat with distant others, however, it is normal that the fear of poisoning should increase, and, as a result, the willingness to overcome that fear becomes a proof of a commitment that is continually being bargained about in the process of establishing moral social links. This seems to be the case in the Zafimaniry example and in the other cases alluded to in this chapter. Thus, very basic aspects of the human condition would account for the cultural recurrences that this chapter illustrates.

Here, however, we must sound the usual note of caution that the discovery of semi-universals always requires, and that was discussed above. The cultural forms and meanings of commensality are varied and therefore no universal human predisposition can fully or directly account for them. At the same time, it would be ridiculous to close our eyes to such strong regularities. Perhaps the kind of model suggested by Dan Sperber (1996) is the most appropriate here, whereby we explain the regularities we have found in terms of the fact that certain representations are merely particularly catching. This would be because they match general human predispositions, without these predispositions being the *source* of the representations themselves. This source having to be found, in part, in the different histories of the different groups concerned, hence the differences. All this is therefore speculation, but speculation that, I believe, could be a fruitful source of further questions and research.

NOTES

1. There is a common French saying implying that if you drink from someone else's glass you will know their thoughts.
2. Miller et al. 1998 show systematically that the points discussed in this chapter apply to the United States.
3. I am only concerned here with terms of address.
4. For the purpose of this chapter, I am ignoring affinity as it would take too much space. However, it should be included in this discussion and would fit in well. Thus, this idiom of kinship, which wants to see all relations in terms of elementary families, hides yet another fact of which the Zafimaniry are only too aware. This is that the continuity of the family, or, to put it in their terms, the survival of the house of a couple through its children, grandchildren, great-grandchildren and so on..., is only possible through the taking in of strangers, as wives of the men, and through separation as the daughters leave to become other men's wives. On a daily basis, however, this is papered over by the parent-child idiom and so a man will call his daughter-in-law or son-in-law 'daughter' and 'son' respectively, and this will apply equally to these in-laws' siblings and so on for all their families.
5. This excludes the descendants of slaves, but this fact is often glossed over.
6. This theme needs much more expansion than is possible here.
7. This is especially true of siblings.
8. The best conductor of closeness is, therefore, rum. The exception is honey, which creates closeness but neutralizes poison. The reason has probably something to do with the fact that honey implies hierarchy whereas rum implies equality.

REFERENCES

Astuti, R. 1994. 'Invisible Objects: Mortuary Rituals among the Vezo of Western Madagascar', *Res* 25.

Bloch, M. 1992a. *Prey into Hunter. The Politics of Religious Experience*, Cambridge: Cambridge University Press.

—— 1992b. 'What Goes Without Saying' in A. Kuper (ed.), *Conceptualising Society*, London: Routledge.

Carsten, J. 1997. *The Heat of the Hearth*, Oxford: Oxford University Press.

Feeley-Harnik, G. 1981. *The Lord's Table*, Philadelphia: University of Pennsylvania Press.

Freeman, J. 1958. 'The Family System of the Iban of Borneo,' in J. Goody (ed.) *The Developmental Cycle in Domestic Groups*, Cambridge: Cambridge University Press.

Hugh-Jones, S. 1996. 'Bonnes raisons ou mauvaise conscience?', *Terrain* 26.

Lévi-Strauss, C. 1966. *Du Miel aux cendres, mythologiques 2*, Paris: Plon.

Miller, L., A. Fiske and P. Rozin. 1998. 'The Social Meaning of Sharing Food in the United States', *European Journal of Social Psychology 28*: 423–36.

Muxel, A. 1996. *Individu et mémoire familiale*, Paris: Nathan.

Sperber, D. 1996. *Explaining Culture*, Oxford: Blackwell.

Trankell, I.-B. 1995. *Cooking, Care and Domestication*, Uppsala Studies in Cultural Anthropology, Uppsala: Acta Universitatis Upsaliensis.

Vialles, N. 1994. *Animal to Edible*, Cambridge: Cambridge University Press.

CHAPTER 5

WHAT IS PASSED ON FROM PARENTS TO CHILDREN

A CROSS-CULTURAL INVESTIGATION

Maurice Bloch, Gregg E. A. Solomon and
Susan Carey

Research from many quarters supports the existence of *core knowledge* (Carey and Spelke 1996). Core knowledge has the following hypothesized properties: (1) its acquisition is supported by innate, domain-specific learning mechanisms; (2) it develops early, under conditions of wide variation in input; and (3) it remains constant throughout development. These three hypothesized properties have the consequence that core knowledge should be cross-culturally universal.

Evidence from human infants (and even non-human primates, see Hauser and Carey 1998) suggests that there are at least three domains of core knowledge: intuitive psychology, with intentional agent at its centre (Gergely et al. 1995; Gopnik and Meltzoff 1997; Johnson, Slaughter and Carey 1998); intuitive mechanics, with physical object at its centre (Leslie 1994; Spelke et al. 1995); and intuitive mathematics, with natural number at its centre (Dehaene 1997; Wynn 1992). Those who are committed to the existence of core knowledge consider it still open whether intuitive biology, with animal or living thing at its centre, is also a core domain of knowledge (for 'yes' see Atran 1998; Keil 1992; Weilman and Gelman 1992; for 'no' see Carey 1985, 1995).

Some argue for core knowledge of intuitive biology on the basis of evidence for an early developing (by age 3 or 4 years), cross-culturally universal, essentialist construal of human and animal kinds, grounded in a folkbiological understanding of innate potential (Atran 1998; Gelman and Hirschfeld 1996; Gelman and Wellman 1991; Horobin 1997; Keil 1992; Rosengren et al. 1991; Springer 1999; Taylor 1996). According to these authors, some human and animal kinds (e.g. species, race, ethnicity, occupation) and some properties (e.g. spoken language, skin colour, properties of internal organs) are considered to be fixed at birth and inherited from birth parents. (Any essential property, constant throughout the life cycle, will be fixed at birth. At issue here is biological inheritance.) Hirschfeld (1995, 1996) suggests that this system of thought contributes to cross-culturally universal construals of race.

An essentialist construal of human and animal kinds is logically independent of its grounding in a folkbiological understanding that essences are inherited from birth parents. Indeed, a great deal of convergent evidence suggests that it is not until the age of 6 or 7 years that a majority of American children have an intuitive understanding of the biological inheritance of properties or of kind. It is not until this age that most children reliably judge that offspring will resemble their birth parents in bodily characteristics and their adoptive parents in beliefs (Johnson and Solomon 1997; Morris 1998; Solomon et al. 1996; Springer 1996; Weissman and Kalish 1999). It is not until this age that most children judge that an animal which looks like a raccoon but has skunk parents and skunk babies is a skunk, not a raccoon (Keil 1989). And it is not until this age that most children reliably judge that offspring will have an unusual property (e.g. a pink rather than a red heart) if their parents were born with it, but not if their parents obtained it by accident (Solomon and Johnson 2000; Springer and Keil 1989). Indeed, Carey (1985, 1995) argues that the developing child's construction of a biological construal of inherited essences requires conceptual change, and thus is not part of core knowledge (see also Johnson and Carey 1998).

Here we focus on the putative cross-cultural universality of a folkbiological essentialism with respect to an individual's properties. Atran (1998) reviewed evidence for cross-cultural universality of certain aspects of species taxonomies and argued that the Itzaj Maya also have an essentialist construal of species kind. But Atran provided no direct evidence that the Itzaj Maya themselves have such an essentialist construal, let alone that they have a folkbiological understanding of the inheritance of physical properties or species kind. Jeyifous (1992) presented unschooled Yoruba children with the Keil (1989) transformation scenarios in which they are asked whether an animal from one species can be changed into an animal from another. She found that Yoruba children treat the task much as do American children, attaining adult intuitions at around 7 or 8 years of age. However, younger Yoruba children, like younger American children, base their judgements of species kind on relatively superficial bodily and behavioural characteristics rather than on aspects of the individual animal's history, including its birth lineage.

Furthermore, there is a large anthropological literature on kinship systems that puts the hypothesis of cross-cultural universality of folkbiological essentialism, based on innate potential, in doubt. In questioning whether all kinship systems are predicated on biological relationships, many anthropologists have come to believe that not all cultures consider birth to be privileged in the mechanisms by which people acquire the properties they do, and that not all cultures construe human kinds essentially.

ANTHROPOLOGICAL BACKGROUND

Kinship studies have traditionally been thought of as at the core of anthropology. The most common reason given to explain that fact is that kinship systems articulate social structure in traditional societies and remain an important element of all forms of social organization. Kinship is thus often seen as the 'natural' anchor on which diverse social systems are grafted. Such an argument requires that what is meant by kinship be, at its core at least, the same everywhere. However, such a theory is now very much in question. An important arena of recent anthropological debate concerns precisely the question of just how deep are cultural differences in kinship systems. These debates focus on a challenge to the many suggestions by the classical authors of anthropology that the constitutive elements of the elementary family, or at the very least the mother-child relationship, are seen to be the same by all human beings and are therefore, in their fundamental aspects, not culturally negotiable.

The debate over variation in kinship systems was taken as central to the discipline of anthropology because it was assumed that the nature/nurture controversy was at its core. Thus, the question was always how much the natural world or how much culture constrained people's understandings.

The possibility that there might be cognitive constraints on how nature was perceived was simply not considered. On the whole, earlier anthropologists implicitly took for granted that parent/child relationships were the building blocks of all kinship systems, and that, apart from discussions over the extent to which the relationship between fathers and children was understood (which was only thought to be a problem for a very few, very primitive societies), they assumed that the parental link was always understood in the same way. Of course, anthropologists were fascinated by differences in the patterns of kinship. For example, they discussed *ad nauseam* the fact that in some cultures members of descent groups are recruited patrilineally, whereas in others they are recruited matrilineally. But these differences were attributed to a cultural choice between links to fathers and links to mothers and not to a different conceptualization of what it was to be a parent or a child. This, it was taken for granted, was always the same. This implicit assumption united very different anthropological traditions, the British social anthropology of Radcliffe-Brown (1924), the American cultural anthropology of Murdock (1949), and the French structuralism of Lévi-Strauss (1949). These traditions probably also made converging assumptions about what was thought to be the cause of such universality, though this was rarely discussed directly. It seems that the various authors simply assumed the link of parent to child was a fact about human biology and that, therefore, this was how all peoples had always seen it to be.

It was only in the 1960s that this faith in a cross-culturally universal understanding of the basic biological relation between parent and child was first contested. The most familiar criticisms are the challenges of Needham (1971) and Schneider (1984). Although different in tenor, they share two elements. First, they pointed out that the biological facts do not 'speak for themselves' but can quite reasonably be understood in a variety of ways, and secondly, they argued that different cultures do indeed understand them differently. They suggested that there is no such thing as kinship cross-culturally since the various systems which have been baptized by this name, although ostensibly involving ideas about procreation, actually evoke fundamentally incompatible representations. The grand comparative enterprises of kinship systems, which so much concerned their predecessors, were merely examples of people adding apples and pears. Needham and Schneider characterized the implicit argument of the earlier anthropologists as being based on a fallacy concerning folkbiology. For kinship to be comparable across different cultures it must be based on the same folk understanding of the relation of parent to children. But, because a wide, perhaps infinite, range of different spins is placed on nature by different cultures, folkbiologies of the relation between parents and children are fundamentally different and incommensurable. The earlier writers had not seen this because they had simply assumed that the folkbiology of the exotic peoples they had studied would be consistent with the folkscientific understanding of biology of the West.

Needham (1971) and Schneider (1984) argued that the anthropological record illustrated very different representations of kinship. The kind of cultural variation that they suggested might exist was that resemblances between parents and children might be believed to be due to such things as that they might have eaten similar food, lived in similar environments, been under the influence of the same supernatural beings, and so on. They suggested that the different cultural explanations involved different mixtures of these elements. In some cultures, one of these elements might also happen to correspond to a (Western) biological notion of the relation of parents to children, but the argument was that each culture has its own recipe for combining these elements and it would simply be a misrepresentation to forget this.

One of the most radical examples of a different cultural explanation of the relation of parents to children is that found in the ethnography of Southeast Asia and Madagascar. The point made by a number of authors: Fox (1987) for the Indonesian world, and Astuti (1995a, b), Bloch (1993), Lambek (1994), Middleton (1995), Ravolomanga (1991) and Southall (1986) for Madagascar – has been that, while in European and African systems, birth and parenthood seem to be the determinant factor in creating fundamental kinship identities, in Southeast Asia and Madagascar, birth is more like, as these people say, 'the launching of a ship'. Where that ship will go will be determined later by other factors such as choice, association and environment. Kinship affiliation will be settled only late in life, and settled definitely perhaps only some considerable time after death.

Accompanying such a view of kinship in these places is the idea that the person, even in bodily characteristics, is continually being made and remade by the kind of things which the individual will learn and practise, and through intercourse with the persons with which the individual associates through life. This malleability has struck most modern anthropologists of Madagascar and they have often noted the fact that Malagasy will often tell you things such as their bone structure is like it is 'because they are fishermen', or they used to belong to a particular ethnic group, but since they have given up the typical activities of that group, they have lost that affiliation, or that their children have whiter skin because they spent a lot of time associating with a French missionary. This malleability due to environment is particularly evident in the case of children who are spoken of as soft and not yet 'finished'.

ON SOME RELATIONS BETWEEN THE PSYCHOLOGICAL AND THE ANTHROPOLOGICAL DEBATES

The debate in psychology over what are innately supported aspects of a framework theory of biology, especially over whether an understanding of biological inheritance is such an aspect, has direct relevance to the current debate in anthropology over the universality of the basic building blocks of systems of kinship. In turn, the anthropological claim of fundamental cultural variation over such matters is obviously a challenge to some of the claims of the psychological literature. However, it is striking how little the practitioners of the two subjects have attempted to put their theoretical proposals together. Many anthropologists who believe that they have demonstrated that culture can construct the world in different ways seem to forget that there might be regularities in representations caused by constraints originating in the nature of the human brain, and they also seem not to consider how their traditional methods of research might mislead them. Many psychologists, on the other hand, seem content to make universalist claims on the basis of studies carried out in only one culture, or in different but closely related cultures, and they seem not to consider some of the methodological difficulties of fieldwork. Clearly there is a need for psychological questions about how it is that a naive understanding of biological inheritance is acquired, to be addressed through cross-cultural research with peoples whose explicitly articulated beliefs on the subject would appear to be very different from those of the West. It is also necessary for anthropologists to check their claims of cultural relativity by using methods which will satisfy sceptics in other disciplines.

The methods of anthropology and the methods of the experimental study of cognitive development are strikingly different. Anthropologists interested in folk-understandings of biological inheritance might observe relevant behaviours and seek explicit explanations for them, and might conduct open-ended ethnographic interviews with native informants (e.g. do pregnant women seek certain experiences and avoid others, and do they explain this behaviour in terms of their effects on the child to come?). In contrast, a developmental psychologist studying young children might look at patterns of forced-choice judgements designed to tap implicit knowledge. For example, a variety of researchers have presented young children with adoption stories and asked whether infants born to one couple would, when grown, come to resemble their birth parents or their adoptive parents in a variety of properties (e.g. Hirschfeld 1996; Solomon et al. 1996; Springer 1996; Weissman and Kalish 1999). At least by age 6 or 7 years, and perhaps earlier, most American children provide differentiated responses, judging that an adopted child will resemble its birth parents in bodily traits such as hair colour or properties of internal organs, and will resemble its adoptive parents in beliefs, preferences, temperaments and skills. Thus, at least implicitly, young American children recognize that distinct causal processes are involved in the fixing of bodily traits on the one hand, and psychological traits on the other.

It is possible that the different conclusions which anthropologists and cognitive psychologists seem to be proposing might simply be due to their different methods. If that were so, it would mean that the conflict in findings is illusory, but also, and perhaps more interestingly, that the two disciplines tap different but coexistent types of knowledge, both of which must be taken into account when we want to characterize what people know.

The present study is the first cross-cultural exploration using the developmental methods developed to tap intuitive beliefs about how individuals come to have the particular properties they do (see also Astuti 2000 and Mahalingam 1998). We study children and adults who belong to the cultural area which is often characterized as Zafimaniry. Ethnographic work shows that the Zafimaniry believe that children come to resemble their parents, in great part, because of the house they grew up in, the environment in which they live, and the people with whom they have interacted (Bloch 1993). The existence of a theory of the acquisition of features that is so different from that of the West offers a test case for the questions which both anthropologists and psychologists seem often to have avoided.

The explicit, articulated beliefs of the Zafimaniry concerning how individuals come to have the properties they do are at variance with the putatively cross-culturally universal folkbiological theory of inheritance, which is acquired by American children at least by age 6 or 7. To explore whether Zafimaniry children and adults share the intuitive understanding tapped by the methods used by developmental psychologists, the procedures of Solomon et al. (1996) were adapted for use in Madagascar. If an essentialist construal of individual people is part of core knowledge, and either includes or leads to the early construction of a folkbiological understanding of inheritance of properties from birth parents, then we would expect the judgements of the Zafimaniry participants to reveal the same differentiated patterns as those observed among American participants. If, in contrast, an understanding of biological inheritance is a cultural construction, as the anthropological literature suggests, then, because the explicit Zafimaniry belief system is so different from that in the West, we would also expect the patterns of judgements of both children and adult Zafimaniry to differ from those obtained in the West.

METHOD

Participants

The study was carried out in 1996 in a remote mountain village in the Zafimaniry area of Madagascar where the basis of livelihood is shifting cultivation and occasional wage work. The population is culturally close to the Betsileo and Merina people of the central plateau. The research was conducted entirely in the local Malagasy dialect by Maurice Bloch, who has been working in the region for more than twenty years and is well known to the villagers. The 7 adults who participated in the study were all over 16 years of age, the 11 older children were between 11 and 15 years old, the 14 younger children were between 7 and 10 years old. Children under 6 years of age were not tested because the researcher found them to be very shy and he reasoned that they were not likely to provide meaningful responses. The village is in a relatively isolated location and the children tested were, to all practical purposes, unschooled (Bloch 1984).

Procedure

The study was a variation on the Solomon et al. (1996) adoption task, and in broad outline the designs are the same. Participants were told the following story about a child born to one couple and raised by another:

> There was a doctor couple who lived in a big town and did not have any children. Here is the picture of the house of the doctor. One day when they were going for a walk in the countryside they saw a numerous group of children playing together. They were the children of a peasant couple. The doctor couple went to the house of the peasant couple and they asked them if they would be willing to give them a child to bring up. There was a newborn child in the peasants' house and the peasants said to the doctor couple that they could bring him/ her up. Here is the picture of the peasants' house. The doctor couple took the child and loved him as though he was their own child and they blessed him. Here is the picture of the child. The child loved the doctor couple too. And now the child is grown up and he still lives in the house of the doctor couple. Now there are a few things I would like to ask you about this story. (See Appendix for the Malagasy original.)

The participants were then asked a series of questions in which the birth parents were described as having one of a pair of features (e.g. straight hair) and the adoptive parents were described as having the other feature (e.g. curly hair). The participants then judged which parent the child would be more likely to resemble on that feature. As in Solomon et al. (1996) the 14 feature pairs were divided among 5 types of trait: 4 bodily traits, 2 beliefs, 3 preferences, 3 skills, and 2 temperaments (see Table 5.1). Participants were encouraged to explain their responses.

Transferring the test to Madagascar involved not only translating the stories and questions of Solomon et al. (1996), but also changing aspects of the story and test items to make them more culturally appropriate for the Zafimaniry. The story was modified so that the families were that of an urban doctor ('doctor' means any medical person with some sort of training) and that of a poor rural peasant, thereby introducing elements concerning class and the rural/urban contrast that were not present in the American study. The notion of adoption in the Western sense does not exist in rural Madagascar though a procedure rather like Western

Table 5.1 Feature pairs used in story, in order in which they were presented

Trait type	Adoptive parent	Birth parent
1 preference	likes oranges	likes pineapples
2 bodily	skin whitish	skin darkish
3 temperament	smooth and calm	angers easily
4 skill	does not know how to plait mats	knows how to plait mats
5 belief	there are birds under water	there aren't birds under water
6 bodily	tallish	shortish
7 preference	likes dogs	likes cats
8 belief	there are little worms in teeth	there aren't little worms in teeth
9 skill	bad at elementary maths	good at elementary maths
10 temperament	not cheerful	cheerful
11 bodily	lightish red blood	darkish red blood
12 preference	does not like songs on the radio	likes songs on the radio
13 bodily	curly hair	straight hair
14 skill	bad speechmaker	good speechmaker

adoption occurs in sophisticated urban contexts. A kind of fostering/ adoption is, however, common in rural areas, but this transfer of children normally occurs between close relatives and is never final. This is called *Mitaiza,* which means literally 'to bring up'. Normally an arrangement such as the one above is only considered if the couples are related, though perhaps quite distantly. In this story the class difference is used in part to make the story credible but also to distance the biological and adoptive parents maximally.

Some of the features pairs used in Solomon et al. (1996) were also changed. As the Zafimaniry were not assumed to be familiar with traffic lights, skunks, Western ovens, baseball, pickles, movies and the like, the traits included such beliefs as believing that there are birds living under water or that little worms live in people's teeth (both of which some Zafimaniry believe to be possible) or such preferences as liking the songs on the radio or such skills as knowing how to plait mats. Despite these differences between the American and the Malagasy versions of the task, the rationales behind the tasks remain the same: the adoption stories allow the biological and social notions of parenthood to be disentangled, and the traits allow participants the opportunity to reveal an understanding that family resemblances on different sorts of trait (such as on bodily traits and beliefs) are driven by different sorts of causal processes.

RESULTS

Judgement patterns

The participants were characterized according to their individual judgement patterns. As in Solomon et al. (1996), the *differentiated* pattern, the pattern most consistent with the explicit folkbiological understanding in the West, is defined according to the participant's judgements concerning bodily traits and beliefs, because it is these two types of trait for which distinct causal mechanisms most clearly underlie their acquisition (i.e. offspring are taken to resemble their birth parents on bodily traits due to biological inheritance, and they are taken to resemble their adoptive parents on beliefs due to learning). The other traits – temperaments, preferences and skills – were included for exploratory purposes, although, as noted above, American participants providing differentiated judgements tend to judge these traits as they do beliefs; the offspring will resemble the adoptive parent.

The *differentiated* pattern was here defined as the pattern in which the child was judged to resemble its birth parents on 3 or 4 of the 4 bodily traits and on neither of the 2 beliefs. A participant had a probability of .08 of showing such a pattern by chance. As in Solomon et al. (1996), those participants who did not provide *differentiated* patterns showed *adoptive parent bias* patterns, *birth parent bias* patterns or *mixed* patterns. Those showing an *adoptive bias* pattern judged the child to resemble its adoptive parents on 11 or more of the 14 traits. This is the pattern most consistent with explicitly articulated Zafimaniry beliefs about how an individual's traits are fixed. Those showing a *birth bias* judged the child to resemble its birth parents on 11 or more of the 14 traits. A participant had a chance probability of .02 of producing either an *adoptive* or *birth bias* pattern of judgement. Finally, patterns that fell into none of the above types were categorized as *mixed*. The number of participants at each age who produced each pattern of judgement is shown in Table 5.2.

The first striking finding is that four of the seven Zafimaniry adults produced a *differentiated* judgement pattern. Just as do American adults, they judged the child to resemble its birth parents on most or all of the

Table 5.2 Number of participants from village who showed each judgement pattern, by age in years

	7–10	11–15	16+
Differentiated	1	2	4
Adoptive parent bias	8	5	0
Birth parent bias	0	0	1
Mixed	5	4	2

bodily features and on none of the beliefs. The strength of this finding is partly masked by the individual pattern analysis reported in Table 5.2. All of the adults, even the one who showed a *birth bias* and the two who showed *mixed* patterns, judged the child to resemble the birth parents on a greater proportion of the bodily traits than beliefs. (The adults who did not show a *differentiated* pattern judged the child to resemble its birth parents on an average of 50 per cent of the bodily traits and only 17 per cent of the beliefs.) Thus, despite the cultural weight the Zafimaniry place on nurture and lifetime events in determining an individual's properties, most adults would appear to understand that resemblance on bodily features, but not beliefs, is mediated by causal processes associated with birth. They would appear to understand biological inheritance.

In contrast, very few of the Zafimaniry children showed the *differentiated* pattern: only one of the fourteen younger children and only two of the eleven older children. Rather, Zafimaniry children's judgement patterns tended to be that predicated on the explicit Zafimaniry belief system concerning how individuals come to have their particular properties. The modal judgement pattern for the children was the *adoptive parent bias* pattern, shown by 57 per cent of the younger children and 45 per cent of the older ones. No children provided a *birth bias* pattern, and the remaining children gave *mixed* responses. Furthermore, of the children who did not show a *differentiated* pattern, only about 32 per cent of the bodily traits were judged to be like those of the birth parent as compared with 23 per cent of the beliefs. Most of the children did not appear to be close to making the categorical distinction between the inheritance of different kinds of trait, though some of the children undoubtedly were in the process of constructing just such an understanding.

As is the case with American participants, the Zafimaniry judged skills, preferences and temperaments much as they did beliefs (see Table

Table 5. 3 Percentage of features of each type judged to be like that of birth parent, collapsing across age

Judgement pattern	Trait type				
	Bodily	Beliefs	Preferences	Skills	Temperaments
Differentiated (n = 7)	90	0	20	5	14
Adoptive parent bias (n = 13)	12	4	5	8	0
Birth parent bias (n = 1)	100	50	67	100	100
Mixed (n = 11)	45	41	45	58	41

5.3). For those Zafimaniry who had shown either a *birth* or *adoptive bias* pattern this was an expected finding, for, by definition, these participants had judged either that the child would resemble its birth parents on virtually none of the traits or on virtually all of the traits. It had also been expected that the Zafimaniry showing the *mixed* pattern would judge the skills, preferences and temperaments as they did the beliefs and bodily traits (and indeed, roughly 50 per cent of all traits were judged to be like those of the birth parents), for overall their judgements did not systematically associate one kind of trait with a particular parent but appeared instead to reflect a variety of strategies. Most interestingly, all seven Zafimaniry with *differentiated* patterns, children and adults alike, were more likely to judge that the child would resemble its adoptive parents in skills, temperaments and preferences, just as they do with beliefs but not bodily traits. Even though the *differentiated* pattern is defined according to judgements on beliefs and bodily traits alone, American and Zafimaniry children and adults who give *differentiated* responses make the same kinds of judgements on preferences, skills and temperaments. This convergence lends credence to the conclusion that the *differentiated* pattern reveals similar understanding across the two cultures, a conclusion bolstered by an analysis of participants' explicit justifications for their judgements.

Justifications

Participants were encouraged to explain their responses. Their justifications provide further information concerning their reasoning in this task. Following Solomon et al. (1996), explanations were coded as *Birth-origin*, *Nurture*, *Teleological*, *Like Birth Parent*, *Like Adoptive Parent*, and *Other*. Birth-origin explanations explicitly invoked the fact that the peasant couple gave birth to the child and so contrasted with the adoptive couple, or implicitly appealed to birth as the origin of the trait. Examples include 'Because he was born to the peasant', or 'Because he got the blood from the peasant'. Nurture explanations referred to the parents' social role or to a specific teaching or learning mechanism. Examples include 'Because he was taught', and 'Because the doctor is the one who brought him up'. Teleological explanations invoked the truth or greater desirability of one of the features. Here the participant is not reasoning in terms of family resemblance, but simply stating that the child would acquire the more desirable trait, leaving the mechanism unstated. Examples include 'Because there really are birds who live under water', or 'Because pineapples taste better'. Like Birth Parent and Like Adoptive Parent explanations explicitly restate which parent the child would resemble, but do not fill in any details of the mechanism. Any explanation not fitting into one of the above categories was coded Other. The explanations were independently coded by two experimenters (GS and SC) who were blind to which participant had produced each one. Intercoder reliability was 95 per cent. Disagreements were resolved over drinks.

Tables 5.4a and 5.4b show the percentage of participants in each judgement pattern who made explanations of each type at least once. Children and adults are presented separately, making it clear that the differences between those participants with *differentiated* patterns and others hold in both age groups. One adult (a *differentiated* pattern) was not asked for explanations and so is not included in Table 5.4.

The justifications given by the *differentiated* participants confirm that they had invoked causal mechanisms to explain family resemblance on bodily traits, which are distinct from those invoked for the other types of trait. Of the *differentiated* children and adults, 84 per cent appealed to Birth-origin explanations at least once in justifying their judgements. Only one of the participants with other judgement patterns ever did so, an adult with a *birth bias* pattern. Furthermore, all of the Zafimaniry who showed the *differentiated* pattern used the Birth-origin justifications only to explain why the child would resemble its birth parent on bodily traits, and not to explain resemblance on any other kind of trait. The adult with the *birth bias* pattern used Birth-origin justifications to explain why the child would resemble its birth parent both on a bodily trait and on a temperament (i.e. angers easily).

Table 5.4a Percentage of 7- to 15-year-olds who made explanation of given type at least once, by judgement pattern

Pattern group	Explanation type					
	B	N	T	LB	LA	X
Differentiated (n = 3)	67	100	0	67	67	0
Adoptive parent bias (n = 14)	0	43	21	43	50	7
Birth parent bias (n = 0)	–	–	–	–	–	–
Mixed (n = 8)	0	0	38	50	25	13

Table 5.4b Percentage of adults who made explanation of given type at least once, by judgement pattern

Pattern group	Explanation type					
	B	N	T	LB	LA	X
Differentiated (n = 3)	100	67	33	100	67	0
Adoptive parent bias (n = 0)	–	–	–	–	–	–
Birth parent bias (n = 1)	0	0	0	100	100	0
Mixed (n = 2)	0	0	50	100	50	100

Key to explanation abbreviations: B = Birth-origin; N = Nurture; T = Teleological; LB = Like Birth parent; LA = Like Adoptive parent; X = Other.

Similarly, 84 per cent of the *differentiated* children and adults appealed to Nurture explanations at least once in justifying their judgements. Moreover, these *differentiated* participants only gave Nurture justifications to explain why the child would resemble its adoptive parent in beliefs, temperaments, preferences or skills, never to explain resemblance on bodily traits. By contrast, only six (24 per cent) of the participants who did not show the *differentiated* pattern ever gave Nurture explanations, and all six had shown *adoptive bias* judgement patterns. Yet, it is striking that even for these participants who favoured resemblance to the adopting doctor, the Nurture justifications were only given to explain resemblance on beliefs, temperaments, preferences or skills. Contrary to the ethnographic literature, the Zafimaniry participants, whether or not they had demonstrated an understanding of biological inheritance, did not appeal to Nurture explanations to explain how the child would acquire such bodily features as skin or blood colour.

Teleological explanations were provided by eight participants, distributed widely over age and judgement pattern. All of the teleological justifications, which appeal to the truth, the intrinsic preferability or the desirability of a feature, were only given for beliefs, preferences, temperaments or skills, and never for bodily traits. This result suggests that these justifications were implicit Nurture explanations, that the child would end up acquiring the skills, beliefs and preferences of the culture. It further suggests that though many of the participants may not have constructed an understanding of biological inheritance, they understand that the kinds of factor implicated in the acquisition of beliefs, skills and preferences are not also factors in the acquisition of bodily traits.

Finally, a large number of the justifications were not informative. Participants in all judgement patterns often said that the child would have some property because it would be like the peasant (the birth parent) or because it would be like the doctor (the adoptive parent, or 'bringer up' as one would say in Malagasy). These Like Birth Parent and Like Adoptive Parent justifications may implicitly reflect appeals to distinct causal mechanisms for fixing traits, or they may simply be restatements of the resemblance judgements or general appeals to family resemblance without any underlying causal process in mind. In support of the latter possibility, we note that 50 per cent of the participants who showed *non-differentiated judgement* patterns appealed to Like Birth Parent justifications for bodily traits, but that 29 per cent used the same justification for the other traits as well. Similarly, 33 per cent of the Non-Differentiated participants appealed to Like Adoptive Parent justifications for bodily traits, and 54 per cent did so as well for the other traits. Finally, the uncodable Other explanations were given rarely, once each by only four of the participants.

The *differentiated* pattern, justified by explicit appeals to Birth-origin and Nurture explanations and by Teleological explanations offered only for non-bodily traits, reflects an understanding of the biological inheritance of bodily features, in contrast to environmental forces or learning processes that cause other types of trait. The *adoptive parent bias* pattern may have two different sources: such a judgement pattern could reflect a participant's belief that specific post-birth environmental factors are responsible for the creation of most of a person's properties, or the pattern could simply reflect the two-step reasoning that a child will resemble its parents and that the relevant parents are those who bring the child up. The justifications suggest both sources were operative, although specific Nurture explanations were never given for bodily traits. Similarly, the *birth parent bias* pattern may reflect beliefs in the biological inheritance of most of a person's properties, or simply that a child will resemble its parents and the biological father and mother are the relevant parents. The adult who produced the sole *birth bias* pattern was likely engaging in at least some of the former type of reasoning, given that he produced explicit Birth-origins justifications for both a bodily trait and a temperament. Finally, *mixed* patterns reflect a pattern of reasoning not organized around the contrast between family types.

CONCLUSIONS

The ethnographic literature on Southeast Asia and Madagascar in general, and the Zafimaniry in particular, describes articulated beliefs about how an individual person's properties are fixed. The present study was designed to elicit patterns of judgement reflecting implicit understandings of biological inheritance. The pattern of judgements most consistent with the ethnographic literature is one in which an adopted child is said to resemble its adoptive parent rather than its birth parent on most traits, and in which such judgements are justified by Nurture or Teleological explanations. The study yielded two important results: first, not a single Zafimaniry adult participant provided data consistent with what would have been predicted from the ethnographic literature alone. Rather, more than half performed as would American adults on this task. One participant judged that the child would resemble its birth parent on almost all traits, and the remaining two gave *mixed* responses. These data reveal an intuitive understanding of the fixation of bodily traits by a process that implicates innate potential and the fixation of the other traits by a process that implicates learning and social factors.

The second important result is that Zafimaniry children, between ages 7 and 15, were different from the Zafimaniry adults. Only a few provided *differentiated* patterns, and most of the others showed little sign of distinguishing the processes through which bodily features and beliefs are fixed. Rather, their modal response pattern, the *adoptive bias* pattern, was that predicted by the ethnographic literature.

Despite the Zafimaniry's consistent, explicitly articulated beliefs concerning a person's malleability during development, over half of the adult participants (and even some of the children) displayed the *differentiated judgement* pattern that reveals typical Western folkbiological understanding. It seems likely that the conflict between the picture of Zafimaniry beliefs about parent/child resemblance that derives from ethnographic research and the picture that derives from the present study reflects differences in methodology. The conflict is real, and is seen within individual informants. One of the adults who produced a *differentiated response* pattern in the peasant/doctor scenario also assured one of us (MB), in another context, that because on a previous visit to the village he had ridden in a car with a pregnant woman, the woman's child, now a 2-year-old, looked like him, was white like him and walked like him. Further research is needed to systematically explore the meaning of this conflict. It seems likely that different modes of explanation coexist. The symbolic function of each mode of explanation and the contexts in which each is elicited remain to be elucidated. But what seems clear, subject to confirmation by further research, is that the explicit Southeast Asian anti-essentialist picture of people as in the process of 'becoming' all their lives is not incompatible with a folkbiological understanding of the inheritance of certain properties from one's birth parents.

In many ways this study should be seen as a pilot study. Only one version of the story was given to all participants, and the sample sizes, especially of adults, were small. However, subsequent work by Astuti (2004) on the Vezo of Madagascar provides striking converging data to those reported here. The Vezo make statements similar to those of the Zafimaniry concerning the malleable nature of young children and the role of practice in fixing physical and non-physical properties of an individual. Yet, in a slightly different version of a similar adoption story, 78 per cent of thirty-one Vezo adults provided *differentiated* responses.

Astuti also confirmed that most children (ages 6 to 13) did not provide *differentiated* responses, as only 12 per cent of forty children did so. However, in one way, Astuti's results differ from ours. Whereas the Zafimaniry children were likely to show adoptive biases, the Vezo children were more likely to show birth biases (30 per cent) than adoptive biases (18 per cent). Both patterns were statistically systematic; that is, Zafimaniry children provided more *adoptive bias* patterns than would be expected by chance and the Vezo children provided more *birth bias* patterns than would be expected by chance. We have no explanation for the different patterns of responses. Perhaps the Zafimaniry cultural story of the lifelong process of 'becoming', or 'hardening' one's personal characteristics, more saliently supports an adoptive bias. Alternatively, the difference may be due to the fact that the Zafimaniry are even more isolated from Western culture than are the Vezo.

Whereas the present data may be of surprise to anthropologists who believe that folkbiological understanding of the consequences of the fundamental parent/child relationship displays radical cross-cultural variation, they also hold no comfort for those who believe that an understanding of biological inheritance is part of core knowledge. Apparently, the folkbiological theory of inheritance of properties revealed by adoption and switched-at-birth scenarios does not develop early and spontaneously under widely different conditions of input. In this study, most Zafimaniry children below age 16 did not display it, a result confirmed by Astuti's (2004) Vezo sample. This is in marked contrast with American children, who provide *differentiated* responses by age 6 or 7 in versions of these experiments as close to the present one as we could manage. Further research is needed to explore several possible factors that might contribute to the striking differences between Zafimaniry children and American children. For example, Zafimaniry children are largely unschooled, and thus may be less likely than American children to respond to the pragmatic demands of the structure of this task (Cole and Scribner 1974). If so, then less demanding versions of the present task (e.g. Springer 1996; Hirschfeld 1996; Solomon 1996) may reveal earlier understanding among Zafimaniry children. It is also likely that the Zafimaniry children's responses reflected the influence of the explicit Zafimaniry beliefs about how people come to have whatever traits they do. It is striking that Zafimaniry children never produced *birth bias* patterns, even though these are common among American and Vezo children in the process of working out a differentiated account of the fixation of individual people's traits (Solomon et al. 1996).

These results bear directly on Hirschfeld's (1995, 1996) claims for a cross-culturally universal, early-developing, essentialist construal of race, grounded in a theory of innate potential. The bodily property of skin colour, a stand-in for race in Hirschfeld's own switched-at-birth and adoption scenario, was one of the four bodily properties probed in this study. Among non-*differentiated* children (88 per cent of the sample), the child was no more considered to resemble its birth parent in skin colour than its adoptive parent. As noted in our introduction, essentialist construals of race, ethnicity, species kind and individuals' properties are logically distinct from their being grounded in folkbiological understanding of inheritance. The present study is consistent with other evidence (Carey 1995; Solomon 1996) that such folkbiological understanding is acquired slowly during childhood, and may even require conceptual change.

Given that Zafimaniry adults display the differentiated understanding of biological inheritance tapped in this task, why are Zafimaniry children so slow to develop it? Why do the Zafimaniry children differ so much from the Zafimaniry adults? One possibility is that the Zafimaniry adults, at least some of them, had the benefit of much better schooling than do current Zafimaniry students, given the deterioration of the Malagasy economy. As suggested above, better schooling helps a participant analyse the relevant contrasts in the task (in this case, two types of families, two types of traits). Or, more directly, the Western folkbiological understanding might have been taught in school. If the difference between Zafimaniry children and adults is due to better schooling of the latter, then totally unschooled adults from this culture should not display differentiated understanding on such tasks. Further research could explore this possibility. Consistent with this type of explanation for the difference between Zafimaniry children and adults in the present study is the observation that Zafimaniry children are not expected to declare their solutions to intellectual problems – indeed, they are openly ridiculed if they hold forth about serious matters – they may have been less apt to engage the adoptive/biological problem we put to them and instead may have interpreted the task superficially and so fallen back on the ready-made explanations provided for them by their culture. We have no evidence that this is in fact the case, but simply note it as a logical possibility.

A second possibility is that, because of the existence of such ready-made and culturally significant explanations for how an individual's properties are determined, children are less apt to try to seek out alternative explanations. They are less apt to find themselves in the kind of explanatory quandary that has been implicated as a major factor motivating conceptual change and the construction of new frameworks of understanding (Bromberger 1992; Kuhn 1977; Solomon and Johnson 2000). Despite the likelihood that Zafimaniry children have far more occasions to witness sex and birth in animals as well as in humans, they need not have recognized the kinds of distinction and covariation that would undermine the culturally-provided theory. Indeed, the bias against seeking out or even recognizing disconfirming evidence is a well-documented, almost certainly universal, phenomenon (Wason and Johnson-Laird 1972). If the construction of an intuitive theory of biological inheritance requires conceptual change, such conceptual change must await relevant input and motivation. Zafimaniry adults have constructed such a folkbiological theory. We can only speculate as to what the motivation and input might be that would lead Zafimaniry adults and not children to engage in conceptual change; perhaps it is not until parenthood that one naturally wonders why a child looks the way it does.

Why, then, does the construction of a differentiated intuitive biological theory of inheritance occur so early in American children? First, American children are not faced with an explicit belief system at variance with this construal. Second, American adults' explicit folkbiological understanding of how each individual's properties are fixed is consistent with the *differentiated* pattern probed in this scenario. And third, the distinction between biological and adoptive families is salient in American culture, and even in young children's experience. Thus, even if the construction of an intuitive biological theory of inheritance requires conceptual change, by age 6 or 7 it is not unlikely that American children will have encountered the input and motivation needed to achieve it.

The results from the Zafimaniry, at the very least, highlight the dangers of psychological generalizations based on data from a single culture and of anthropological generalizations which assume that the 'knowledge' of a particular group of people can be accessed unproblematically through what is said in the type of contexts which normally satisfy ethnographers.

ACKNOWLEDGEMENT

The authors thank Rita Astuti, Fatemeh Khosroshahi, Dan Sperber, and the Fondation Fyssen for their support.

APPENDIX. ADOPTION STORY (MALAGASY VERSION)

Nisy mpivady mpitsabo izay mitoetra any an-tanan-dehibe tsy manan-janaka Ity ny sarin-tranon'ireo mpitsabo. Nefa maniry mafy ny hitaiza ankizy. Indray andro raha sendra nitsangatsangana tany ambanivohitra izy ireo dia nahita ankizy maro nilalao. Izay mpamboly ny ray amandrenin'ireo ankizy ireo. Nandeha tany an tranony izy mivady mba hifampidinika aminy, fa manam-pikasana ny hitaiza ny iray amin'ireo ankizy ireo. Nisy zaza voa teraka tao ka io zaza io no nomen'ireo mpamboly ho taizan'ireto mpitsabo. Ity ny sarin-tranon'ireo mpamboly. Io ny sarin'ilay zaza. Nanome toky izy ireo fa hotiaviny toy ny izany io zaza io, ka nitsodrano ilay zaza izy ireo. Amin'izao fotoana izao dia efa lehibe io zaza io, izay mbola mipetraka ao amin'ireo mpitsabo. Misy zavatra manintona anao tao amin'io angano io.

REFERENCES

Astuti, R. 1995a. *People of the Sea Identity and Descent among the Vezo of Madagascar*, Cambridge: Cambridge University Press.

———. 1995b. 'The Vezo are not a Kind of People: Identity, Difference, and "Ethnicity" among a Fishing People of Western Madagascar', *American Ethnologist* 22: 464–82.

———. 2001. *Are We All Natural Dualists?: A Cognitive Developmental Approach*, *Journal of the Royal Anthropological Institute* 7: 429–447.

Astuti, R., G. Solomon and S. Carey. 2004. *Constraints of Conceptual Development*, Monographs of the Society for Research in Child Development, No. 277. Vol. 69.

Atran, S. 1998. 'Folkbiology and the Anthropology of Science: Cognitive Universals and Cultural Particulars', *Behavioural and Brain Sciences* 21: 547–609.

Atran, S., D. Medin, E. Lynch, V. Vapnarsky, E. Ek and P. Sousa. 2001. 'Folkbiology Doesn't Come from Folkpsychology: Evidence from Yukatek Maya in Cross-cultural Perspective', *Journal of Cognition and Culture* 1: 3–42.

Bloch, M. 1984. 'Knowledge, Literacy and Schooling among the Zafimaniry of Madagascar', in B. Street (ed.), *The Anthropology of Literacy*, Cambridge: Cambridge University Press.

———.1993. 'Zafimaniry Birth and Kinship Theory', *Social Anthropology* 1, 119–132.

Bromberger, S. 1992. *On What We Know We Don't Know: Explanation, Theory, Linguistics, and How Questions Shape Them*, Chicago: University of Chicago Press.

Carey, S. 1985. *Conceptual Change in Childhood*, Cambridge, MA: Bradford Books.

——, 1995. 'On the Origin of Causal/Explanatory Notions', in D. Sperber, D. Premack and A. Premack (eds), *Causal Cognition: A Multidisciplinary Debate*, Oxford: Clarendon.

Carey, S. and E. Spelke. 1996. 'Science and Core Knowledge', *Philosophy of Science* 63: 515–33.

Cole, M. and L. Scribner. 1974. *Culture and Thought: A Psychological Introduction*, New York: Wiley.

Dehaene, S. 1997. *The Number Sense: How the Mind Creates Mathematics*, New York: Plenum.

Fox, J. 1987. 'The House as a Type of Social Organisation on the Island of Roti', in C. Macdonald (ed.), *De la hutte au palais: Sociétés 'à maison' en Asie du Sud-Est insulaire*, pp. 171–8, Paris: CNRS.

Gelman, S. and L. Hirschfeld. 1999. 'How Biological is Essentialism?' in D. Medin and S. Atran (eds), *Folkbiology*, Cambridge, MA: MIT Press.

Gelman, S. and H. Wellman. 1991. 'Insides and Essences: Early Understandings of the Nonobvious', *Cognition* 38: 213–44.

Gergely, G., Z. Nadasdy, C. Gergely and S. Biro. 1995. 'Taking the Intentional Stance at 12 Months of Age', *Cognition* 56: 165–93.

Gopnik, A. and A. Meltzoff. 1997. *Words, Thoughts and Theories*. Cambridge, MA: MIT Press.

Hauser, M. and S. Carey. 1998. 'Building a Cognitive Creature from a Set of Primitives', in C. Allen and D. Cummings (eds), *Evolutionary Psychology and Epistemology*, Oxford: Oxford University Press.

Hirschfeld, L. 1995. 'Do Children have a Theory of Race?', *Cognition* 54: 209–52.

——. 1996. *Race in the Making. Cognition, Culture, and the Child's Construction of Human Kinds*, Cambridge MA: MIT Press.

Horobin, K. 1997. *Children's Understanding of Biological Inheritance: Nature, Nurture, and Essentialism*. Paper presented at the biennial meeting of the Society for Research in Child Development, Washington, DC.

Jeyifous, S. 1992. 'Developmental Changes in the Representation of Word Meaning: Cross-cultural Findings', *British Journal of Developmental Psychology* 10: 285–99.

Johnson, S. and S. Carey. 1998. 'Knowledge Enrichment and Conceptual Change in Folkbiology: Evidence from Williams Syndrome', *Cognitive Psychology* 37: 156–200.

Johnson, S., V. Slaughter and S. Carey. 1998. 'Whose Gaze will Infants Follow? The Elicitation of Gaze-Following in 12-month-olds', *Developmental Science* 1: 233–38.

Johnson, S. and G. Solomon. 1997. 'Why Dogs have Puppies and Cats have Kittens: The Role of Birth in Young Children's Understanding of Biological Origins', *Child Development* 68: 404–19.

Keil, F. 1989. *Concepts, Kinds, and Cognitive Development*, Cambridge, MA: MIT Press.

———. 1992. 'The Origins of an Autonomous Biology', in M. Gunnar and M. Maratsos (eds), *Modularity and Constraints in Language and Cognition: The Minnesota Symposia on Child Psychology, Volume 25*, Hillsdale, NJ: Erlbaum.

Kuhn, T. 1977. *The Essential Tension*, Chicago: University of Chicago Press.

Lambek, M. 1994. *Body and Mind in Mind, Body and Mind in Body: Thought, Practice, and Incommensurability*. Paper presented at the annual meeting of the American Anthropological Association.

Leslie, A. 1994. 'ToMM, ToBy, and Agency: Core Architecture and Domain Specificity', in L. Hirschfeld and S. Gelman (eds), *Domain Specificity in Cognition and Culture*, New York: Cambridge University Press.

Lévi-Strauss, C. 1949. *Les Structures élémentaires de la parenté*, Paris: Presses Universitaires de France.

Mahalingham, R. 1998. 'Essentialism, Power, and Representation of Caste: A Developmental Study'. Unpublished doctoral dissertation, University of Pittsburgh.

Middleton, K. 1995. 'Tombs, Umbilical Cords and the Syllable Fo', in S. Evers and M. Spindler (eds), *Cultures of Madagascar: Ebb and Flow of Influences*, Leiden: International Institute for Asian studies.

Morris, S. 1998. 'The Development of Children's Naive Theories of Biology'. Unpublished dissertation, University of New South Wales, Sydney, Australia.

Murdock, G. 1949. *Social Structure*, New York: Macmillan.

Needham, B. 1971. 'Remarks on the Analysis of Kinship and Marriage', in R. Needham (ed.), *Rethinking Kinship and Marriage*, London: Tavistock.

Radcliffe-Brown, A. 1924. 'The Mother's Brother in South Africa', *South African Journal of Science* 21: 542–55.

Ravolomanga, B. 1991. 'Pour la beauté et la santé de l'enfant à naître', in S. Lallemand et al. (eds), *Grossesse et petite enfance en Afrique Noire et à Madagascar*, Paris: L'Harmattan.

Rosengren, K., S. Gelman, C. Kalish and M. McCormick. 1991. 'As Time Goes by: Children's Early Understanding of Growth in Animals', *Child Development* 62: 1302–20.

Schneider, D. 1984. *A Critique of the Study of Kinship*, Ann Arbor: University of Michigan Press.

Solomon, G. 1996. 'Race and Naive Biology'. Unpublished manuscript.

Solomon, G. and S. Johnson. 2000. 'Conceptual Change in the Classroom: Teaching Young Children to Understand Biological Inheritance', *British Journal of Developmental Psychology* 18: 81–96.

Solomon, G., S. Johnson, D. Zaitchik and S. Carey. 1996. 'Like Father, Like Son: Children's Understanding of How and Why Offspring Resemble their Parents', *Child Development* 67: 151–71.

Southall, A. 1986. 'Common Themes in Malagasy Culture', in C. Kottak, J. Rakotoarisoa, A. Southall and P. Verin (eds), *Madagascar, Society, and History*, Durham NC: North Carolina Academic Press.

Spelke, E., A. Phillips and A. Woodward. 1995. 'Infants' Knowledge of Object Motion and Human Action', in D. Sperber, D. Premack and A. Premack (eds), *Causal Cognition: A Multidisciplinary Debate,* Oxford: Clarendon.

Springer, K. 1996. 'Young Children's Understanding of a Biological Basis for Parent-Offspring Relations', *Child Development* 67: 2841–56.

——. 1999. 'How a Naive Theory of Biology is Acquired', in M. Siegal and C. Peterson (eds), *Children's Understanding of Biology and Health*, Cambridge: Cambridge University Press.

Springer, K. and F. Keil. 1989. 'On the Development of Biologically Specific Beliefs: The Case of Inheritance', *Child Development* 60: 637–48.

Taylor, M. 1996. 'The Development of Children's Beliefs about Social and Biological Aspects of Gender Differences', *Child Development* 67: 1555–71.

Wason, P. and P. Johnson-Laird. 1972. *Psychology of Reasoning Structure and Content*, Cambridge: MA: Harvard University Press.

Weissman, M. and C. Kalish. 1999. 'The Inheritance of Desired Characteristics: Preschoolers' Beliefs about the Role of Intention in Biological Inheritance', *Journal of Experimental Child Psychology* 73: 245–65.

Wellman, H. and S. Gelman. 1992. 'Cognitive Development: Foundational Theories of Core Domains', *Annual Review of Psychology* 43: 337–75.

Wynn, K. 1992. 'Addition and Subtraction by Human Infants', *Nature* 358: 749–50.

CHAPTER 6

A WELL-DISPOSED SOCIAL ANTHROPOLOGIST'S PROBLEMS WITH MEMES

Maurice Bloch

Memes are a wonderful teaching device for the student who wants to learn about human beings *in general*. They serve as a clear and imagination-stimulating concept for the beginner who needs to understand what makes human culture so very different from types of behaviour that are directly genetically driven. Furthermore, talking of 'memes' bypasses the trap of making culture seem transcendental, mysterious and immaterial. The concept of memes thus avoids the Scylla of sociobiology – which fails to take into account the radical specificity of the human mind and what it implies – and the Charybdis of the dualisms of much philosophy and social science – positions that ultimately refuse to accept human knowledge as a natural phenomenon. This is the right epistemological starting point for those who want to engage in the adventure of anthropology.

The final chapter of Dawkins' *The Selfish Gene* on memes is, therefore, an excellent, general, well-written introduction to the subject of culture. But it also attempts to do something which is much rarer and particularly valuable. It presents matters in a way that makes the reader realize that biologists and social scientists are specialists dealing with different parts of what is ultimately a unitary phenomenon. These different kinds of scientist therefore have to have theories that are congruent. Nonetheless, the difficulties they often have in understanding each other are not simply due to separate styles and traditions, but to fundamental features of the different bits of the single totality they are engaged in studying.

There have been many previous attempts at cooperation between natural and social scientists, but they have usually failed because of the crudest misunderstandings of either the nature of the social and the cultural by natural scientists or of the biological and psychological by social scientists. Meme theory deserves a better fate, yet I am afraid the story so far has not been encouraging. Indeed, we have to note how little success the concept of memes has had among social scientists. The great majority of sociocultural anthropologists would not even recognize the word and, when it is explained to them, they are invariably hostile. The reasons are various and include sheer prejudice for anything remotely 'scientific', as well as a suspicion that any 'biologizing' of culture rapidly becomes a legitimization for racism and sexism. (It is easy to disregard this as being a case of ignorant self-righteousness, but the history of the subject shows that such fears are not wholly unfounded.) Some other difficulties, however, are caused by a lack of understanding of the work of anthropologists by memeticists. The aim of this chapter is to show what some of these failures are, in order to show why memes, as they are presented, will not do. My purpose, however, is to further the kind of dialogue initiated, or reinitiated by Dawkins, so that this type of general enterprise, will, at a future date, be more successful.

MEMES AND THE ANTHROPOLOGIST'S CONCEPT OF CULTURE

I noted above that, in many ways, Dawkins' work on memes – and that of other writers who have followed him, such as Dennett – is a good, accessible introduction to what is intrinsic in social and cultural anthropology. This fact, however, will not necessarily endear memetics to anthropologists. *At a general level,* Dawkins and Dennett make very similar, if not identical, points to those which anthropologists have always made about human culture. Thus, in the late nineteenth century, Tylor – although an enthusiastic admirer of Darwin and the founder of academic anthropology in Great Britain – stressed how the potential of the evolved human brain meant that the transmission of information between people had become possible in a new way, through symbolic communication, and that this new way meant that human history had a different character to the history of other animals (Tylor 1881, Ch. 1 and 2). Similarly, the concept of 'culture' – usually attributed to the founder of modern American anthropology, Boas, and which notion became the core of the subject in that country – is, in its fundamental implications, identical to the idea of memes (Stocking 1968; Kuper 1988, 1999). Again, the classic American anthropologist Kroeber, at first a pupil of Boas, similarly characterized culture as 'the superorganic', meaning that it reproduces in a way that is independent of the reproductive system of the carriers (Kroeber 1952).

Memeticists should therefore not be surprised at the exasperated reaction of many anthropologists to the general idea of memes. Biologists would react in the same way, if, for example, they were told by a sociologist in 1999, ignorant of Darwin and Mendel, that she had made the following great discovery: that acquired characteristics in animals and plants were not biologically transmitted to the next generation, but rather that there were discrete replicating units of molecular material that were passed on to offsprings. Further, she was going to call these units of transmission 'closets', by association to the verb 'to close', in order to stress the oddity of the fact that these units do not merge and mix into each other in the process of reproduction.

This analogy is a little unfair, but only just. The memeticists could, with justification, reply that memes have an advantage over the usual anthropologist's understanding of culture in that talking of memes stresses the difference with genes, but also reminds us that this does not mean that we have, for all that, left the natural world behind. After all, such formulations as Kroeber's 'superorganic', referred to above, rapidly lead to various forms of implicit dualisms. Such mystifications have been and, once again these days, are particularly common in anthropology. It is one of the virtues of the meme idea that it guards against this temptation in a way which, nonetheless, retains the core of the culture concept. This is true, but we should not forget that many anthropologists have made the same point in a variety of ways, and were able to do this without ever having heard of memes (for example Steward 1955, White 1959, Harris 1968, Godelier 1984 and Lévi-Strauss 1962). Furthermore, such an epistemological stance – although rarer than it used to be – has not been silenced by such fashions as postmodernism, with its scientific allergies, and appears in a variety of forms in recent publications (see Bloch 1998, Sperber 1996, Carrithers 1992, and many others). The detractors of anthropology, who want to argue that we are all out-and-out dualists, seem always to go back to the same old examples of extreme relativism (which they commonly misrepresent) in order to legitimate their contempt for the subject (Pinker 1998; Blackmore 1999). But, as they do this, they ignore the great majority of anthropological work, which they simply do not know or have heard of at second- or third-hand. Of course, it is difficult to keep up with the literature in other disciplines, not to say one's own, but memeticists have freely chosen to explore *exactly* what anthropologists have been studying for more than a century. As a result, they have no excuse for not finding out what the discipline has to offer. To use an analogy once again: a social scientist who, for some reason, chose to write about photosynthesis, would not be justified in pleading lack of time for not acquainting herself with the botanical literature.

The first point to stress is, therefore, that emphasizing the many dramatic implications of the fact that the evolution of the human brain has meant that information can replicate, persist and transform by means other than DNA is very valuable. The notion of memes does perform this function for a biological audience, perhaps ignorant of anthropology. But this point has already very often been made by anthropologists.

FALLING INTO OLD TRAPS

Repeating what has already been said in other words can be useful, especially if the point is particularly important. This is the case with some of the discussion of memes. If memes were only a new way of talking about what anthropologists have meant by culture, the lack of acknowledgements would still be annoying to us, but the educational value of the enterprise would remain. If memeticists want to stress the difference between the transmission of information through genes and memes, then they are in step with traditional anthropology. However, it is obvious that this is not all there is to memes. They also want to stress a fundamental *similarity* between memes and genes. The similarity lies in the fact that memes and genes, although made of different substances, both replicate and are therefore subject to the Darwinian algorithm (Dennett 1995). This inclusion of culture and biology within the same framework has a positive aspect, which I have stressed above, but the particular similarity emphasized by the memeticist, I argue, is wrong and misleading. Furthermore, it is wrong and misleading in a way that could have easily been avoided if memeticists had been more concerned with anthropology. The problem which anthropologists immediately recognize with memes lies not so much with the very *general* idea, but with a specific aspect of the theory: the notion that culture is ultimately made of distinguishable units which have 'a life of their own'. Only then would it make sense to argue that the development of culture is to be explained in terms of the reproductive success of these units 'from the memes' point of view'.

Bits of culture?

Memetics implies that human culture is made of discrete bits. This is suggested by the analogy with genes. As with genes, finding out exactly what units are involved has proved – even for the most enthusiastic supporter – difficult to define. But, clearly, this analytical isolation has to be somehow demonstrated, even if such a task is seen as a provisional enterprise needing much future refinement. The reason why this *has* to be done with genes is that the very basis of the modern evolutionary synthesis would be incomprehensible without there being distinct genes which can replicate and be selected for independently of each other. To use Dawkins's famous title, it is necessary for genes to have a 'self' to be 'selfish'. For the same reason, if, following Dennett and others, we are to believe that the same evolutionary algorithm governs meme and gene selection, memes have to be something with a defined existence in the world; they cannot remain an arbitrary unit of analysis, created merely to talk conveniently about the world, but with no clear ontology. There is no real doubt about the ontology of genes. Of course, this does not mean that the nature and boundaries of genes are beyond dispute. But it is clear what kind of things they are claimed to be, and scientific advances have made their existence plausible. Again, this does not mean that genes have to be totally independent from each other. We know that genes form clusters and that this clustering affects the selective potential of each gene. But to talk of clusters also implies that we believe in the separate existence of the constituents. Thus, no modern geneticist would seriously maintain that the genome is a totally seamless continuum, which could equally legitimately be divided up in any way that took the fancy of a particular scholar. Now, if the idea of memes is legitimate, the same rule should apply to culture, that whole formed by memes: it too cannot be a continuous entity. The memeticist must believe that there ultimately *are* discrete memes on which natural selection acts, whether these form clusters or not. The memeticist will most probably recognize that different aspects of culture (memes) are linked and that this will affect the selective history of the units. This is what they mean when they talk of memeplexes. But again, such an idea obviously also requires that the units be somehow objectively distinguishable, even though associated into -plexes.

The question is: is this a reasonable way to represent the knowledge of people – in other words their culture? Is it made up of distinguishable bits? As I look at the work of meme enthusiasts, I find a ragbag of proposals for candidate memes, or what one would otherwise call units of human knowledge. At first, some seem convincing as discrete units: catchy tunes, folk tales, the taboo on shaving among Sikhs, Pythagoras' theorem, etc. However, on closer observation, even these more obvious 'units' lose their boundaries. Is it the whole tune or only a part of it which is the meme? The Sikh taboo is meaningless unless it is seen as part of Sikh religion and identity. Pythagoras' theorem is a part of geometry and could be divided into smaller units such as the concept of triangle, angle, equivalence, etc.

Matters become even more difficult when we turn to such much more typical and important phenomena as, for example, a traditional farmer's knowledge about the weather. It is impossible to convincingly demonstrate that this is made up of a number of actually existing, finite number of discrete bits. How many bits would it include? Is the belief that certain types of cloud are an indicator of hail separate from the knowledge that hail damages crops? Memeticists would perhaps then want to speak of 'memeplexes', but they are no more able to establish boundaries around these memeplexes than around the constituent memes. Is the practice of finishing the main rounds of rituals during the rainy season because the ancestors have so ordained and because the harvest can only take place when the crops are dry, is it a part of the memeplex about the weather, or the religion memeplex, or the naive physics memeplex, or the social memeplex? Or is it that all these things link up into one gigantic memeplex? The answer to these questions can only be totally arbitrary. In reality, culture simply does not normally divide up into naturally discernible bits.

The Coherence of culture

This fact raises two fundamental issues. The main one, to which I return in the next section, is the ontological status of memes. The other is the question of the coherence, or otherwise, of culture. To this I now turn.

Whether culture is coherent is at the very heart of what has been, for more than a century, a key theoretical controversy – perhaps the most important and difficult source of anthropological polemics. A mass of writing and research has argued over this question and, although anthropologists are far from any agreement, at least we know what kind of arguments need to be taken into account and why the issue is so difficult. This awareness is what seems to be lacking in the discussion on memes, again probably because memeticists have not bothered to acquaint themselves with this work.

A simplified account of the history of anthropology would be as follows. The subject appeared in the academy at the end of the nineteenth century, largely in the wake of the initial enthusiasm caused by Darwin's work. At that time, the discipline saw its role as filling the gap in our knowledge about what happened between the emergence of *Homo sapiens* and the beginning of writing, at which point historians were to take over. The early anthropologists were encouraged by Darwin but hardly Darwinian in any precise sense. In fact, they tended to be guided by a much older tradition, which saw the history of humankind as going through a series of 'stages' which had to be passed through in order to reach 'civilization'. Archaeology was to provide information about these earlier times and so too were living non-Western peoples because these were, so it was believed, still 'at an earlier stage'. These stages were usually characterized in a variety of ways, often by their technology. It was thus assumed that, if a contemporary group of people lived by hunting and gathering, studying them would yield information about the early history of mankind, when our ancestors were all hunters and gatherers. This kind of assumption is, of course, still quite common today, not least among sociobiologists, evolutionary psychologists and even memeticists (Blackmore 1999: 195).

However, this type of reasoning soon ran into three very great difficulties. The first is that modern hunters and gatherers live in conditions quite unlike those of our ancestors, precisely because they are surrounded by non-foragers. This means that it is unlikely that what goes for contemporary groups of hunters and gatherers applied also in the past. The second difficulty is that nobody has convincingly shown that such things as religious systems and the technology of food production are closely linked. Thus, modern hunters and gatherers have all kinds of totally different religious systems, and we cannot therefore infer what our ancestors believed in, simply because they were not agriculturalists. Third, the time elapsed since the emergence of *Homo sapiens* is identical for New Guinea highlanders and the people who work on Wall Street; the history of both groups has been equally long, varied and complex. There is absolutely no reason to believe that the New Guinea highlanders have somehow been frozen in time and are thus 'living fossils' retaining unchanged the customs of thousands of years ago. We know their history sufficiently well to see that this is simply not so.

These by now familiar difficulties were not, however, the points that the main critics of anthropological evolutionism picked on immediately after the 'evolutionist' period. These early twentieth-century writers chose instead to emphasize that cultural traits *diffused* from person to person, and from society to society. These critics, often enthused by a desire to counter the impious implications of all forms of evolutionism, thus embarked on great enterprises of tracing the geographic itinerary of particularly 'catchy' bits of culture; these they called 'traits' and founded a number of so-called diffusionist schools, such as the *Kultur Kreise* school in Germany, the 'children of the sun' school in Britain, and the American 'culture contact school' to which many disciples of Boas belonged. The principal occupation of these groups was tracing the migration of these cultural traits.

The basic point was quite legitimate. It is that people do not need to go through all the intermediate stages of technological knowledge to be able to use a computer, for example. One generation may have no idea about electricity, while the next may be innovating a new computer program under Windows. This is not due to a speeding up of 'cultural evolution' but the result of a totally different process: the fact that humans can communicate knowledge to each other. In other words, what goes for biological evolution does not apply to culture because humans transmit information from person to person. As noted above, there were many diffusionist schools and several still exist to a certain extent. Some of these schools were somewhat bizzare; others made points that were accurate and interesting. What they have in common, however, is their central argument that human culture is not to be understood as governed by an evolutionary process. Evolutionary anthropologists of the nineteenth century, such as the famous Lewis Henry Morgan who so influenced Marx and Engels, were therefore wrong, because diffusion meant that history was freed from the bounds of nature. It is therefore ironic that the strongly anti-Darwinian flavour of their stance should be so strikingly similar in form to those of the memeticists. It is therefore also particularly relevant to meme theory to take note of the criticisms which the diffusionists soon had to face. These might be called the 'consistency criticisms'.

Culture is consistent

These criticisms came in two forms. The first, American version – associated with such pupils of Boas as Ruth Benedict (1934) – was much influenced by Gestalt psychology. It stressed how cultures form consistent wholes; how every element – wherever it came from – was moulded to fit in with the others because of a psychological need for integration which led to an organically patterned 'world view'. The second type of 'consistency criticism' is more associated with the British school and is usually labelled 'functionalist', although this label itself covers a range of different positions. It settled down into what we may call the 'British social structural approach' which dominated in much of Europe between 1940 and 1970. This approach stressed that culture was not just a set of mental attitudes and beliefs but mental attitudes and beliefs *in practice:* the practice of living in society. And, since living in society implies coordination and ordered cooperation, mental life cannot be separated from the order impressed on it by the nature of society. In this version, the coherence of mental beliefs and attitudes merely reflects the greater and more imperative need to engage in coherent practices necessitated by social structure (Radcliffe-Brown 1952) – and not, as in the American version, due to a psychological need.

Both these approaches inevitably implied a criticism of the diffusionists' emphasis on the transmission of isolated units. The American version of the consistency criticism stressed that even if a bit of information came from one culture and was adopted by another, this could occur if the trait became, in the process, an inseparable part of the culture pattern into which it was incorporated. It then ceased to exist as an identifiable unit. Furthermore, the process of assimilation means that the original element becomes totally modified, so that it was not any more the same phenomenon it had been in another culture. According to this way of seeing things, if one wants to explain the nature of a trait, its ultimate origin is very largely irrelevant. This is, first, because any incorporated trait accepted by an individual or into a new culture was inevitably modified so as to be coherent with the context. Second, any borrowed trait is not a foreign body with a life of its own, but only exists because it is given life by its incorporation into a new whole. Thus, the fact that the habit of making noodles came to Italy from China does not explain why Italians make noodles. An explanation requires why making noodles seemed, and still seems, right to Italians given their beliefs, symbolism, economy, agriculture and perhaps family organization. This is why Italians want, and do, make noodles. What noodles mean to Italians is therefore quite different from what they mean for the Chinese.

This type of position was further developed, and to an extent criticized, in Lévi-Strauss's version of structuralism. As with the Americans, the need for coherence also originated for him in the human mind. But his view of the patterning process was more rigorous and, above all, more dynamic than in the theory of such writers as Benedict. For Lévi-Strauss, coherence came from the psychological necessity for order, made manifest through specific types of structure (such as tree structures and binary oppositions), which then rendered the combination of units possible. For him, structuring is only the first stage in a generative process in which new forms are continually emerging in a similar way to grammar, whose patterning is merely an enabling device for the production of an infinity of utterances.

The Lévi-Straussian position is taken a step further in the work of Sperber, who distinguishes sharply between the act of transmission or communication on the one hand, and the representations in the minds of the producer of the communication and the person who receives it, on the other. For Sperber, unlike Lévi-Strauss, these mental representations are integrated and produced by a private mental process which is of a quite different nature to the historical process of continual cultural creation.

What the approaches of Lévi-Strauss and Sperber have in common is a relative distancing from the overemphasis on coherent wholes, which characterized the earlier ideas of culture in writers such as Benedict.

They are thus in accord with other recent tendencies in anthropology that stress the variety of voices in society rather than the (unconvincingly assumed) cultural unison of earlier writers.

These several criticisms and modifications of what we may call the 'Benedict programme' of a coherent, consistent cultural realm are important. But they should not make us forget that anthropologists, such as Sperber, Lévi-Strauss and most of their colleagues – as well as myself – accept the fundamental criticisms formulated by the American consistency theorists against the diffusionists: criticisms which apply with equal force against memeticists. Agreement is focused on the fact that the transmission of culture is not a matter of passing on 'bits of culture' as though they were a rugby ball being thrown from player to player. Nothing is passed on; rather, a communication link is established which then requires an act of *re-creation* on the part of the receiver. This means that, even if we grant that what was communicated was a distinct unit at the time of communication, the recreation it stimulates transforms totally this original stimulus and integrates it into a different mental universe so that it loses its identity and specificity. In sum, the culture of an individual, or of a group, is not a collection of bits, traits or memes, acquired from here and there, any more than a squirrel is a collection of hazelnuts.

The British version of the consistency criticism of diffusionism shares many elements with the American version. These aspects of the theory are, however, not the ones which principally concern me here. However, one aspect is particularly relevant to the subject under examination since it applies equally as a criticism of memetics. British social anthropologists are typically uncomfortable with the very idea of culture. As their name implies, they would rather stress the social aspect of human life than the cultural. Thus, during the period when American anthropologists were developing theories concerning the need for culture to be patterned, the British used the stress on the social to criticize the idea of culture on the basis that it was too decontextualized from the *practice* of ordinary life.

This emphasis on action made the British suspicious of the idea that what is shared among members of the same society is like a vast, consistent encyclopaedia of knowledge incorporating definitions, rules, representations and classifications. Of course, British social anthropologists did not, like extreme behaviourists, deny that for social and practical action to take place we clearly have to make use of knowledge – a great part of which is learnt by one individual from another. Nor did they deny that this information was then stored in the mind of the receiver so that such knowledge had to submit to psychological laws. But they also wanted to stress that this knowledge is often implicit; that it does not exist in a vacuum. As a result, it is so intimately implicated in action and interaction that it only exists as a part of a whole, only one aspect of which is purely intellectual in character. To represent culture as a collection of bits of information is thus to forget that most of the time it cannot be separated from practices, to which it relates in a number of fundamentally different ways. As a result, for such writers of the British school as Firth (1964) or Barth (1992), knowledge is of many kinds, occurs at many levels and is never independent of a wider practical context. It is therefore better to consider culture not as a set of propositions but as an only partially conscious resource, or perhaps even as a process used in making inferences which inform action – a process which, in any case, occurs at such a speed as to make it necessarily implicit (Bloch 1998, Chs. 1, 2 and 3).

Further, this type of 'culture', on which inferences are based, is often quite at odds with explicit beliefs declared by the people studied or by those who study them (anthropologists for instance), especially when these base themselves principally on the declarations and symbolic aspects of the behaviour of those they observe (see Dennett 1987). With such an attitude, British anthropologists see culture as existing on many levels, learnt implicitly or explicitly in a great variety of ways (e.g. Leach 1954; Bloch 1998). It is not a library of propositions or memes. This type of argument is principally intended as a criticism of American cultural anthropology, which (as we saw) was itself a criticism of diffusionism. But clearly it also applies to the simple diffusionist idea that culture is made up of 'bits of information' that spread unproblematically by 'transmission', where transmission is understood as a unitary type of phenomenon. British anthropologists, including myself, would argue that knowledge is extremely complex, of many different kinds, and impossible to locate, as though it were of a single type. It is not only integrated in single minds at different levels of what is commonly understood by the word 'consciousness', but also inseparable from action.

CONCLUSION

I have dwelt at length on the criticisms which American and British anthropologists have, in the past, directed against the theories of the memeticists' predecessors: the diffusionists. The reason for such a historical excursion must, by now, be obvious: it is that the arguments rehearsed against the latter seem equally valid as criticisms of memetics. As the American critics of the diffusionists showed, memes, like traits, will continually be integrated and transformed by the receiver of information. They do not spread like a virus but are continually and completely made and unmade during communication. The process of their reproduction is not transmission between passive receptors, as is the case for a computer virus, but active psychological processes occurring in people. That is where life is, not in the bits. Second, as the British anthropologists stressed, culture, and therefore 'memes' – if such things existed – would not be made up of a single isolable type of coded information, which, even for the sake of analysis, could usefully be understood as separate from social life. Rather, it would consist of a variety of types of shared knowledge and coordinations which cannot be understood outside the context of the practice of life; it is something that involves both internal and external constraints and contextualizations. This variety of phenomena means that transmission is of many types and is itself part of practice.

Of course, memeticists will want to argue that they are saying more than the diffusionists ever did and cannot therefore be dismissed in the same way. They will bring up the originality of thinking of the evolution of culture from 'the memes' point of view'. And, of course, they are right, because if they had been able to argue that there *were* such things as memes, this would have been a fascinating new perspective on human history. The point is, however, that they have not succeeded in arguing convincingly – any more than the diffusionists had before them when talking of 'traits' – that there are such things *in the world* as memes. And so, talk of invasion by the 'body snatchers', to use Dennett's delightful phrase, is an idea as intriguing, as frightening and as likely as invasion by little green men from Mars. In other words, if there are no memes, learned discussions about whether their reproductive process is comparable to that of genes and whether their relative fitness can ever become an explanation of particular cultural configuration, is simply beside the point.

This seems an entirely negative conclusion, but it need not be. As we saw, the original stimulus supplied by Dawkins set natural scientists on the path to dealing with the key problems which anthropologists have been grappling with since the inception of the discipline in the academy. This was fruitful because, unlike what is the case for most contemporary anthropologists, it made them seek again an *integrated* theory of human evolution which included culture but which did not refuse its special character. This reflection has moved things on from the natural science side, as the work by a number of writers – not necessarily memeticists – shows. It is unfortunate, however, that these people did not make a serious attempt to find out what had been done before concerning these questions; it would have saved them time.

The role of the social and cultural anthropologists in what should have been this joint enterprise is, however, much more shameful than that of their natural science colleagues. They have simply refused to pay attention to people they considered merely as intruders. If they had, they would have disagreed with the memeticists, as I have done here, but they probably would have been saved in the attempt from carrying on in a way which, with time, has become theoretically more and more vague, pretentious and epistemologically untenable. This chapter is an attempt to clear the decks for the very enterprise which Dawkins and Dennett propose. Let us take up the challenge and reflect on what went wrong.

REFERENCES

Barth, F. 1992. 'Toward Greater Naturalism in Conceptualising Society,' in A. Kuper (ed.) *Conceptualising Society*, London: Routledge.

Benedict, R. 1934. *Patterns of Culture*, London: Routledge & Kegan Paul.

Blackmore, S. 1999. *The Meme Machine*, Oxford: Oxford University Press.

Bloch, M. 1998. *How We Think They Think*, Boulder, CO: Westview.

Carrithers, M. 1992. *Why Humans Have Culture*, Oxford: Oxford University Press.

Dawkins, S. 1976. *The Selfish Gene*, Oxford: Oxford University Press.

Dennett, D. 1987. *The Intentional Stance*, Cambridge, MA: MIT Press.

—— 1995. *Darwin's Dangerous Idea*, London: Penguin.

Firth, R. 1964. *Essays on Social Organisation and Values*, London: Athlone.

Godelier, M. 1984. *L'Idéel et le matériel*, Paris: Fayard.

Harris, M. 1968. *The Rise of Anthropological Theory*, New York: Thomas Crowell.

Kuper, A. 1988. *The Invention of Primitive Society*, London: Routledge.

—— 1999. *Culture*, Cambridge, MA: Harvard University Press.

Kroeber, A. 1952. *The Nature of Culture*, Chicago: University of Chicago Press.

Leach, E. 1954. *Political Systems in Highland Burma*, London: Bell.

Lévi-Strauss, C. 1962. *La Pensée sauvage*, Paris: Plon.

Pinker, S. 1998. *How the Mind Works*, London: Penguin.

Radcliffe-Brown, A. 1952. *Structure and Function in Primitive Society*, London: Cohen & West.

Sperber, D. 1996. *La Contagion des idées*, Paris: Odile Jacob.

Steward, J. 1955. *Theory of Culture Change*, Urbana: Illinois University Press.

Stocking, G. 1968. *Race, Culture and Evolution: Essays in the History of Anthropology*, New York: Free Press.

Tylor, E. 1881. *Anthropology: An Introduction to the Study of Man and Civilisation*, London: Macmillan.

White, L. 1959. *The Evolution of Culture*, New York: McGraw-Hill.

CHAPTER 7

ARE RELIGIOUS BELIEFS COUNTER-INTUITIVE?

Maurice Bloch

Anthropologists are great suppliers to the general public, and to certain philosopher clients, of strange beliefs said to be held by remote people. These seem to furnish raw material for thought experiments concerned with the question: how is it possible to hold such beliefs? Or, in the fashion of Davidson: how can one interpret statements by people who apparently believe such bizarre things about the world? On the other hand, most anthropologists, who have studied remote people and who have been engaged in the practice of understanding those foreign others who say this type of thing in real situations, are keen to stress, often to the very same philosophers, that the strangest thing about strange people is how easy interpretation turns out to be.

One way of dealing with this anomaly, one to which I partly subscribe, has been developed by Sperber (1982) and then greatly elaborated and somewhat modified by Boyer (1994). It consists in questioning the apparent strangeness of these beliefs. This position involves stressing that, before one considers the content of bizarre belief statements, one should consider the pragmatic cues which mark how they are intended to be understood in the real world. More particularly, both writers stress that the many strange belief statements reported by anthropologists, which have employed the time of a number of philosophers, are merely intended as tentative propositions about the world and that some intention of the sort is always pragmatically indicated, if only by the obvious counter-intuitive aspect of the assertions of belief. These statements, it is argued, are really understood, and are intended to be so understood, as if in inverted commas, i.e. as: 'I don't know this on my own authority but I hold it as an intriguing possibility since I have been told this by people whom I have every reason to trust, but, on the other hand, I am not going to drop my mental inverted commas as the proposition remains strange and counter-intuitive to me and I don't want to muddle myself by merging it with what I take as obvious'. Sperber and Boyer then point out that these counter-intuitive propositions are only counter-intuitive in very limited ways and so easily remain overwhelmingly within types of knowledge bounded and formed by human-wide, genetically inscribed predispositions which make us all see the world in a particular way. These authors could support a Davidsonian view of radical interpretation on ethnographical grounds, since all humans, by their common nature, already share so much, and what they do not share is so severely constrained that the problem of radical interpretation would only occur when people meet Martians.

The Sperber–Boyer position further attempts to show that it is precisely the intriguing, indicated, counter-intuitive character which makes religious-like beliefs catchy, so that such beliefs become easily established as part of a shared culture within a given population.

Boyer says that this catchiness explains the weird fact that 'religion' exists, since these counter-intuitive beliefs are, for him, what it consists of. He apparently denies what most anthropologists would now maintain, that there is no such *thing* as religion, other than the somewhat, but only somewhat, similar phenomena one finds in different places, and which remind the observer, in a theoretically insignificant way, therefore, of what we have been brought up to understand by the term (see Bell 2002). He implies that the various counter-intuitive beliefs weave together to create a whole of linked representations and practices.

Boyer and Sperber's ideas about counter-intuitive statements are very important. I entirely support their key point, which is that before we can consider the rationality, or otherwise, of representations, we need to grasp how they are meant to be understood in real situations. Furthermore, they are right when they stress that a number of belief-type statements have often wrongly been taken, by ethnographers and others, as straightforward affirmations about how the world is, while it is clear that their implicatures are of a totally different order. It is probable that such famous cases as the Nuer assertion that 'Twins are birds' (Evans-Pritchard 1956: 77) or 'we are red Macaws' (Crocker 1985) are of this type.[1] Sperber illustrates his position with a story about dragons. He shows how he was, at first, mistaken in taking a request to kill a dragon as the same sort of speech act as a mundane request to carry a basket, for example, while in fact he should have realized the implicit presence of pragmatic inverted commas which marked the statement to be understood as 'far from ordinary'. More recently, Sperber has emphasized his position again by arguing that, come what may and given human innate dispositions to see the world in a particular way, such beliefs can never become intuitive-like (Sperber 1997).

I have no problems with his argument for this example, but I am uncomfortable about how ethnographers can know, in general, when to assume the presence of implicit inverted commas and therefore when to set in motion the 'further scrutiny' deemed necessary for interpretation according to Sperber. He seems to think this scrutiny is triggered simply by the evident counter-intuitive character of the belief, like the switch of register required for understanding a live metaphor brought about by the obviously outrageous character of the statement (see Thourangeau and Sternberg 1981).

The story of the dragon is straightforward, because there is clearly a bizarre element in someone declaring a belief in the existence of dragons for us and, it also turns out, for the people concerned. But what if a statement seems to us apparently odd, but not so to the people concerned? And what if nobody is very clear? Thus I have often been told, by sophisticated Malagasy, something like the following story: 'Europeans go around the country secretly stealing blood, or other vital constituents, from poor people in Madagascar by means of techniques which are those of flying witches; they do this while moving around mysteriously and unseen by everybody. These Europeans then use the stolen bodily elements to diminish the life force of the Malagasy and to increase their own, or that of third parties, usually other rich Europeans, to whom the Malagasy hearts, blood or bones are sold'. Some will also add that they have heard warnings, through a European-sponsored media campaign, intended for the Malagasy, that however poor they are they should have nothing to do with such trade in organs, especially kidneys. Indeed, a Swiss doctor, broadcasting in Madagascar, has been heard on the radio by me and some of my informants, saying precisely this.

Such statements constitute much more awkward examples than Sperber's story about dragons. How much of this story would be treated by an ethnographer working according to the criteria implicitly suggested by Sperber and Boyer, as counter-intuitive? First of all, the part about the trade in organs is very unlikely to be considered by such an ethnographer as an example of the statements she suspects are taken as counter-intuitive and therefore worthy of special treatment. On the other hand, the part about witchcraft-like thefts is likely to arouse this type of suspicion, but both elements are clearly an inseparable whole, at least as far as the informants are concerned. In fact, I, and, I believe on the basis of my empathetic ethnographic observation, they, as hearers of such statements, as well as other recipients, will not be sure how the story is intended by the speaker or intended to be heard by the hearers. Is the speaker claiming that it is something she has heard from others, but that she treats with the greatest of caution because it appears counter-intuitive? After all, removing blood from a person without being seen to do it, or having direct contact with them, or leaving any trace on their body, is extraordinary. Or, on the other hand, is this story treated as a statement of an apparently intuitive fact about the world, passed on through reliable sources, which therefore needs no particular precautions or scrutiny, like my being told by a doctor that I have caught a virus? After all, when people steal things from you, they try to hide what they are doing so you will not be aware of what is happening; if reliable people tell you that such thefts are taking place, there is nothing counter-intuitive in this information. Finally, it is possible that the first time one hears such a story about heart thieves one treats it as odd, but then, subsequently, one hears this story so often that, every time it comes up, it requires less and less critical attention; in the end, it becomes exactly *like* an unexamined intuitive belief, in that its hearsay aspect has been eroded. When information has become as familiar as this, it is no different from being told that if you eat too many unripe fruit you will get diarrhoea – something you may well not have experienced yourself, and for which you have no intuitive connection between cause and effect, but which seems so sensible, given the frequency of the statement and the reliability of the informers, that it is experienced 'as good as'. In the case of the blood and heart thieves story, the confirmation comes from the evident fact that Europeans are richer and healthier than Malagasy peasants for no very obvious other reason.

These indeterminacies of translation seem to me characteristic of much that we find in the field, indeed, they are more typical than Sperber's story about the dragon. How any story will be heard, whether about dragons, blood thieves or stomach aches is an empirical question, which Sperber and Boyer do not address, perhaps because they assume an *a priori* way of knowing what kind of propositions are counter-intuitive in terms of their content. But, if the content is context-dependent and the real contexts are as fluid, as changing and as uncertain as I have suggested, merely declaring a proposition to be counter-intuitive, on the basis of what they acknowledge is a highly speculative psychology, is not sufficient. This does not mean, however, that we should not use, as Sperber and Boyer certainly do, our interpretative intuition and examine such claims critically to analyse what might be happening. But interpretation is only possible in terms of an existing state of affairs where the communication takes place.

THE OLD ANTHROPOLOGICAL PROBLEM WITH 'BELIEF'

There may be another, even more fundamental problem, which lies at the back of all this. This is whether the focus on 'belief', counter-intuitive or not, as the core concern in dealing with religion is not misleading for the type of phenomena under examination. Both Boyer and Sperber have a strong background in anthropology and in the kind of fieldwork from which the 'twins are birds' stories have originated, but I wonder if as a result of trying to address a mainly philosophical audience, they have not forgotten something which we anthropologists teach to our first-year students: that is, that the very stress on 'belief' may be misleading for the kind of religions studied by anthropologists such as myself.

The anthropological challenge to the usefulness of 'belief' for the study of religion has a long history. It was first formulated by Robertson Smith, and subsequently echoed by Durkheim, and explored in depth by such writers as Needham (1972), Pouillon (1979), Lenclud (1990), and others. The problem seems to involve two elements. First, philosophers are interested in the types of mental states roughly indicated by the phrase (in English) 'to believe that', while anthropologists are often concerned with phenomena indicated by the phrase 'to believe in'. Secondly, the phrase 'to believe in' is only appropriate for a particular type of counter-intuitive claim, typical of certain religions, of which Christianity is the most obvious example, where 'to believe in' *should* be, but *is* not, the same as 'to believe that'. Or to put the matter as would a number of philosophers such as Davidson and Dennett, both discussed by Lenclud (MS n.d.), we are not dealing with simple beliefs but with reflexive beliefs on reflexive beliefs to the nth degree.

However, these distinctions, often made by the writers cited above, seem to get forgotten when philosophers and anthropologists enter into a dialogue. That is usually when talk of belief and/or representations and/or interpretation comes to the fore, while the flesh of the context from which this data is issued fades out of sight, becoming forgotten in ethereal thought experiments.

A MALAGASY EXAMPLE

One way to begin to illustrate the problem and discover what might be its origin, is to recount a little of the history of Madagascar in the early nineteenth century (see Bloch 1986: Ch. 2). This was the time when European Christian missionaries arrived on the island. They saw their primary task as demonstrating the errors of 'savage' religion, which they understood as most probably the work of the Devil, and replacing such paganism with true Christian beliefs. However, the missionaries soon found themselves faced with an unexpected problem, created by this very programme. They simply could not work out what were the erroneous *beliefs* the Malagasy held, which they were to counter. They found little that fitted the bill of their understanding of 'primitive', or 'demonic', or 'pagan' religion. The issue was, to a certain extent, resolved when a kind of dialogue was established between the Malagasy and the missionaries, which gradually led them to agree together about what they thought they disagreed about.

The missionaries were led to direct their attention to the *belief* in 'idols' which, they claimed, was held by the Malagasy. As Welsh Calvinist Christians, or as Lutheran Norwegians, whose history had been so centrally concerned with denouncing the idolatry of the 'whore of Rome', and the even more insidious idolatry of the Anglican quislings, this was a very comfortable stance. They had found their golden calf which they could destroy according to a venerable tradition. Once the missionaries had decided that what they were to eradicate were the 'idols', the Malagasy, for their part, at last understood what the Europeans were objecting to with such vehemence – they were against what the Malagasy called *sampy,* the word the missionaries had been led to translate as 'idol'. This word designated objects and cults which were often of foreign origin, and which are referred to in the Africanist literature as 'medicines'. One characteristic of such cults, which are typically imports from outside, is that they are always 'in question'.[2] New 'medicines' were and are continually introduced, others are dismissed as ineffective or harmful. This means that the issue whether one 'believed', or 'chose', or simply tried out a particular medicine was always relevant and no doubt furnished the occasion for statements of the kind: 'I believe you should try this particular medicine and not this one.' The missionaries' attack on *sampy*/idols appeared sensible to the Malagasy also, since it could be understood in this way.

The fact that the missionary–Malagasy dialogue led to the focus on the eradication of *sampy* was to have great historical significance. When the Merina (the dominant group in Madagascar when the missionaries first came) converted to Christianity in the mid-nineteenth century, they duly burned the Idols/*sampy* in great *autos da fé*. It made perfectly good sense since by then, it was agreed all round, this was what was to be changed and replaced by Christianity. But, at the same time, far more important rituals and practices, such as those concerning ancestors, were hardly called into question at all, either by the missionaries or by the Merina Christians. This was because, for the missionaries, these 'beliefs' had an ontological status which looked quite unlike what they expected from 'religion', and, for the Malagasy, the ontology of ancestors was not a suitable subject of reflection. Thus the ancestors were largely ignored; these still continue to be barely challenged by the strong Christian commitments of most present-day ordinary Merina Christians. This fact explains much of characteristic contemporary religious activity in Christian Madagascar, which is accompanied by what looks very much like ancestor worship. It is as though, since the missionaries had not been sure what to say about ancestors, these 'beliefs' were unaffected by conversion.[3]

The nature of the dialogue between the Malagasy and the missionaries and its legacy is thus explicable by two factors, one from either side. The first concerns the nature of Christianity itself. The second is the nature of 'beliefs' concerning entities such as ancestors.

Christianity is a 'believe-in religion'. At least that is how it would be represented by adherents, i.e. believers, who are asked about it. They would say, 'As Christians we believe in...' Thus, the most typical aspect of Christianity, something which it shares to a relative extent with the other Semitic religions, is its stress on the importance of *emphatic* statements of 'belief' of which the creed is perhaps the most obvious example.

It is as though Christians feel so unsure of what they declare that they have to repeat, emphatically and endlessly, what they believe *in,* to convince themselves and others that they believe *that* the world is so, rather like a child coming back home in the dark might repeat to herself 'I am not afraid of the dark.' Christianity seems to say there are things which are so, and are indeed normally *taken* to be so, but that this is not good enough for religion; some extra reflexive and counter-intuitive beliefs have to be added on top and these have to be *taken* as so, in an exaggerated kind of 'belief' act, sometimes called 'faith' (see Pouillon 1979).

The other side of the missionary–Malagasy dialogue concerned the nature of people's involvement with ancestors. What that involvement was, and still is, cannot be known, either from thought experiments or sketchy historical accounts, precisely because of its largely implicit character. Therefore, I have to draw on what I have known through long-term fieldwork as an anthropologist in Madagascar on and off between the 1960s and the 1990s. This is obviously a risky procedure but, given what I know of Madagascar, far less risky than just guessing without any specific ethnographic experience. In ordinary contexts, the Malagasy are simply not interested in whether they, or anybody else, 'believes' in ancestors in the Semitic religions' sense, any more than they are interested in whether they, or anybody, believes in 'fathers'. Indeed, this comparison is particularly relevant since ancestors are treated in ways which are very reminiscent of the way living ascendants are treated. Writing about Africa, Kopitoff (1971) stresses, in a way that would be equally appropriate for Madagascar, that behaviour toward dead ancestors is apparently fundamentally no different than it is toward living fathers or elders. The motivations, emotions and understanding of elders and ancestors are assumed to be the same. Ancestors are simply more difficult to communicate with. Thus, when rural Malagasy, in perfectly ordinary context, want to be overheard by the dead, they speak more loudly, something they often also do when they want elders to take notice, since these are also often deaf. I would not go as far as Kopitoff in saying that there is *no* difference in how ancestors and elders are evoked, especially in rituals, as I shall discuss below, but he is right insofar as, in many ordinary situations, the difference never becomes salient. The ancestors are not as close as living parents or grandparents, but they are not all that distant, and differential closeness is, after all, typical of all kinship systems.

In a similar vein, the famous Chinese anthropologist Fei Xiaotong, also referred to by Bell (2002), writing in the 1940s, describes an encounter with his grandmother's ghost in this way:

> One day not long after her death, I was sitting in the front room looking toward her bedroom. It was almost noon. Normally at that time grandmother would go to the kitchen to see how the lunch preparations were coming along... This had been a familiar sight for me, and after her death the everyday pattern was not changed. Not a table or chair or bed or mat was moved. Every day close to noon I would feel hungry... The scene was not complete without grandmother's regular routine, and so that day I seemed to see her image come out of her bedroom once more and go into the kitchen. (Fei Xiaotong 1989)

In ordinary contexts when one does not really want to involve the ancestors very actively – for example when offering a libation to them before a shared bottle of rum or when asking for their blessing before a minor journey – people's behaviour does not seem to be marked as different, or as concerned with counter-intuitive beings. To implicitly assume the ancestors' existence does not seem to require a special type of effort, as would be necessitated by the understanding of a counter-intuitive proposition. Knowing ancestors, therefore, is not an act of value, or duty or daring, as Christians would claim is the case for Christian belief. Thus, to the Malagasy even today, after total familiarization with a Semitic religion, the idea of 'converting' somebody to a belief in ancestors is ridiculous, like converting them to a belief in the existence of fathers. People are not normally interested in what ancestors are like and, unless pushed very hard by an ethnographer, they have nothing much to say about such things as the way the ancestors spend their time, where they might be located, their way of existence, or how to account for their powers. What does concern the Malagasy are such things as how they can get ancestors to help them and whether ancestors are the agents behind diseases or other unpleasant occurrences happening to them, at a particular time. The ancestors' usual ontological and rhetorical status is no different from that of rain. Normal people, normally, do not take the fact that rain can get one wet as a subject of thought or discourse. Indeed, I suspect they would be at a loss for words to explain how this happens, rather they are concerned whether they will get wet if they go out, now, without an umbrella. Christianity and Islam, on the other hand, seem concerned above all with what humans *do to* God, i.e. believe in him. Malagasy concern with the ancestors is the other way round. What matters is what ancestors *do to* you.

This fundamental difference between the way ancestors are conceived and the way God is conceived in Christianity meant that the missionaries, with their belief-focused religion, could simply not get a grip on ancestors since these were not the kind of phenomena they expected, given the type of religion they knew. They could not convert the targets of their missionizing away from a belief in ancestors, since the Malagasy could not understand what the missionaries were talking about or what they wanted. This explains the fact that many present-day Malagasy, who are clearly devout Christians and who therefore believe that they believe *in* God and in the divinity of Christ and do not believe *in* ancestors, because they know Christians do not, surprise themselves and others by being suddenly involved with ancestors in ways requiring rituals of which they thought they disapproved. The Christian business of belief and disbelief has not given them the tools to address their relation with their dead forebears which is, therefore, 'untouched' by what they consider 'religion'.

On the other hand, something closer to the Christian emphasis on belief was involved with the *sampy,* since the attitude toward them, as it is revealed in social practice and talk about them, was, and still is,[4] one which emphasizes their counter-intuitive nature. I suspect that the missionaries felt not only comfortable, but also relieved, when they hit upon the *sampy* as likely targets for translation, because when they tried to eradicate *sampy* the Malagasy could react to them as sensible people who made sense. After all, this type of attack was familiar and had been going on a long time. People who attacked particular *sampy* were as comprehensible to the Malagasy as someone who tells us that a particular brand of headache medicine we have been using is ineffective and that they have a better one we should try. By contrast, people who attacked the belief in ancestors would be as weird as Martians turning up, trying to convince us that eyes were not true.

DIFFERENT SUPERNATURAL BELIEFS AND DIFFERENT COGNITIVE ATTITUDES

My argument is that Sperber and Boyer are misled in thinking that all religious manifestations are cognitively and saliently counter-intuitive, in the same way the missionaries were misled in only looking for that type of belief. On my reading, when Sperber and Boyer identify the religious with the counter-intuitive, they are unwittingly thinking in the terms of Christian, or Semitic, religions, perhaps because they are addressing interlocutors who know nothing else. I suspect that, if they were considering the Malagasy case, they would rightly have found their type of counter-intuitive in the *sampy* and their cults and also, wrongly, in the ancestors — two types of phenomenon which accordingly they would lump together. The reason why they would not be able to differentiate is that they would not have based themselves, as here, on an approach informed primarily by the nature of the actual evocation of these two very different types of agent in natural situations; something which ethnographic fieldwork enables us to do particularly well.

However, there seem to be a number of related counter-objections to my criticisms of the Sperber–Boyer stance. First, these two authors might well defend themselves by arguing that the taken-for-granted character or familiarity of a belief concerning entities such as ancestors is irrelevant to the attitude people have toward the object of that belief. They might also argue that, if Malagasy people fear diseases sent by the ancestors, which they certainly do, and do things which are *out of the ordinary* to contact them, i.e. perform rituals, then the oddity of this means of communication demonstrates the counter-intuitive nature of ancestors.

Even though ancestors are said to speak, and it is an unchallengeable fact, for the Malagasy, as for anybody else, that dead bodies do not speak, the problem with taking entities such as ancestors as counter-intuitive is that this ignores the usual *attitude* that people display toward the supernatural entities in question. Most speakers of statements about ancestors do not, most of the time, indicate that they are referring to counter-intuitive beings, and, therefore, to interpret their statements as indicating this type of mental state seems unwarranted. To classify ancestors as counter-intuitive beings implies something which is ethnographically wrong: that, *to the ordinary Malagasy,* they are experienced as the same sort of beings, with similar types of attribute, as those evoked in the creed, or, for that matter, belief in particular *sampy.* By ignoring the difference, we would be merging phenomena which, while perhaps superficially potentially cognate in one way (because they seem odd to the ethnographer), could not, as we saw, be more contrastive from the social, cultural, communicative or cognitive point of view. This categorical difference is revealed by the acid test of their differential reaction to history.

The basis of the problem is that a stance which identifies the counter-intuitive with *a priori* characteristics, that can be inferred from the nature of the entities proposed, ignores the role of communicative practice in real situations. This was precisely what Sperber and Boyer were criticizing others for omitting. Furthermore, such an approach ignores the ever-changing evolution of attitudes of people toward these entities through time and in different circumstances. Thus a representation, which a particular person might understand as counter-intuitive when they first come across it, out of the blue, so to speak, clearly does not have the same cognitive significance as it does when it has become totally familiar, and has been held as valid by oneself and everybody else around for as long as anyone can remember.

As an additional problem, the case of an accepted proposition, such as the existence of ancestors for the Malagasy – something never even discussed as an issue or rhetorically marked in any way as peculiar – is totally different from the content of those assertions of belief that are continually marked as being in doubt or out of the ordinary by being prefaced on Sundays with the phrase 'I believe'. In a society such as pre-Christian Madagascar, it is the former state of affairs which is typical of most aspects of the religious, though not all. In fact, the matter may be even more complex, since it may be that some people, all the time, consider the ancestors as counter-intuitive, while other people, all the time, never have an attitude toward the ancestors with a whiff of anything counter-intuitive, and that still other people, some of the time, suddenly feel the statements made about the ancestors to be counter-intuitive while, most of the time, they do not. In fact, for the Malagasy, on the basis of the most anecdotal of evidence, the third case seems to me to be the most common, but this does not mean that the two attitudes are not sharply contrasting.

These fundamental differences in attitude should not be ignored by the Sperber–Boyer-type theories of religion since it is precisely the arresting cognitive presence of the counter-intuitive in certain representations which the two authors see as the explanation of their historical and evolutionary destiny. Thus Sperber and Boyer argue that, if certain representations are counter-intuitive in the way they appear to *the people who hold such representations* (NB not in themselves) then such representations will be somehow stimulating and interesting to entertain, and will then spread and stabilize through the population, becoming part of the culture. But I am arguing that, if the representations they are talking about are, for the people concerned, of totally different cognitive types and seem to display very great differences in degree of counter-intuitiveness, then, their catchiness, or otherwise, will also be totally different. Furthermore, if some of these representations are so familiar as to be just like intuitive beliefs, then the special catchiness attributed to the stimulation of the counter-intuitive will be nullified.

The second objection to my criticism of the Sperber–Boyer theory of religion is somewhat similar and can be phrased as follows. One could argue that, although the Malagasy are not normally much concerned with the ontological status of beings like ancestors on a day-to-day basis, when they want to contact these supernatural entities, for example when they want to ask them to remove a disease which the ancestors have sent, then, by the very act of attempting communication, they expose the counter-intuitive nature of their belief, since such contact cannot be established in the straightforward way one would with regular creatures.

According to this objection, the way such entities as ancestors can be communicated with, in moments when it is really important to do so, contrasts drastically with the way one would communicate with a person, such as a neighbour, with whom one might, for example, engage in a two-way conversation. With dead ancestors, such straightforward reciprocal intercourse is not possible and, instead, exchange must take place through ritual. This fact, it can be argued, must bring to the fore the counter-intuitive nature of ancestors in that what we call rituals are characterized, precisely, by the *oddness* of the means of communication employed. For example, in rituals the typical means/ends rationality of everyday life is abandoned for one that is obscure for all concerned, including the ritual practitioners, were they to be obliged to explain it (which, in normal circumstances, not faced by an ethnographer, they do not have to do) (see for example Leach 1954: 11).

However, on the interpretation I am advancing, ritual, far from enabling the participant to become aware of the intuitive or counter-intuitive nature of the entities addressed, does precisely the opposite. If anything, it is the use of ritual as a means of communication which itself becomes the focus of the awareness of the counter-intuitive element, while the beings evoked in the process almost completely fade from view.

This is because ritual removes the possibility of intellectual discursive evaluation of the forces involved or of the reasonableness of the exact nature of communication. Certain rituals are indeed 'addressed' to the ancestors and so they imply the strange fact that people who are dead get up to things and do these things in unseen and unheard ways, yet the very nature of rituals, as many anthropologists, including myself, have pointed out, involves such actions as singing rather than speaking, such unexplained symbols as lambs and fishes, rather than straightforward signs, and this places them in the category not of semantics but of pragmatics. One cannot be sure whether any proposition in a ritual context asserts anything in particular about the world which, even implicitly, could be taken as either 'intuitive' or 'counter-intuitive'. What makes it reasonable in English to label the acts I am talking about as rituals, therefore, is the out-of-the-ordinary character of the communicative mode they employ, but not the-out-of-the-ordinary character of their semantic content. Rituals involve communicative practices which are *alternatives* to normal understandings and meanings, and which hinder and interfere with the tools we normally think we need to make ourselves understood (and through which we can interpret what we and others believe). One enters a ritual mode of communication by radical modifications of ordinary behaviour. Speech becomes singing, even wordless singing. Customary adaptation of means to end is obscure. The Gricean requirements are nowhere on the horizon. One cures by killing. One often synchronizes one's bodily and linguistic movements with those of others. This is so to the extent that one is not sure whether it is oneself or another inside oneself who is acting and using one's voice and one's body. Thus, in rituals concerned with the ancestors, one floats off in a highly emotive but semantically obscure world; rituals are attempts to achieve this state. One needs to go through the looking glass, but, once there, one loses all reference points. In other words, in the practice of ritual, the cognitive effect of the fact that the ancestors might be counter-intuitive is irrelevant.

There is a further aspect. Rituals cannot, by definition, be spontaneous. They are conventional actions where the intention to mould what one is saying or doing for the sake of transmitting representations is impossible, since the moulding has already been done, long before, by person or persons unknown. The Davidsonian preliminary requirement for interpretation, *viz.* that what the speaker utters is intended by herself to be true, or rather to be understood by the hearer as intended to be understood as true by the hearer, is absent in ritual action, since one cannot identify the originator of the message who might have made such a commitment and whose intentionality could be read. Furthermore, most rituals are done in a group, and so participants find themselves doing, singing or saying things that are willed in part by others, too, and only afterwards can one try to work out what all this 'means'. In other words, linguistic statements of belief concerning the ancestors evoked in rituals, which could be interpreted as counter-intuitive (for example those that anthropologists might succeed in extracting from their informants) are merely *post hoc* reflections or rationalizations of what cannot, by its very nature, be put in ordinary language because it is not an ordinary language matter. Whether these rationalizations are to be interpreted as counter-intuitive or not is irrelevant to the experience itself.

Thus, the phenomenon of the ancestors evoked in rituals is a thousand miles removed from being told intriguing stories about dragons, the choosing *of sampy,* and the implicit or explicit testing of one *sampy* against another. It is a thousand miles removed from saying, in the cold light of morning, perhaps to an anthropologist, 'We are all red macaws', or 'Twins are birds'. This is not to say that this type of reflective activity is unimportant in places like Madagascar or that it never occurs in myth, where the arresting quality of the counter-intuitive representations might well account for its spread. But this is not the case in ancestor worship.

To sum up, the English term 'religion' normally indicates phenomena which imply a consideration of strange 'beliefs' with an explicit and clearly emphasized counter-intuitive element (for example a stress on life after death as a subject of reflection). This is what is salient in general discussions of 'religion' in Euro-America. This is because the particular history of the Semitic religions, especially Christianity, influenced as it was by Platonism, made faith in the not-fully-knowable the touchstone of what religion is (Pouillon 1979: 51). People like the pre-Christian Malagasy do, and did, also have practices focused on stressed counter-intuitive beliefs. But the most important aspects of the kind of thing they did, which we would readily label religion, are simply not there and this fact has enabled it to survive attacks in the name of the alternative 'religion' which Christianity presented itself as. And, therefore, just as it was for the missionaries, discussions of the content of 'the beliefs of the Malagasy', in the European sense of the words, such as might be found in the work of Sperber, Boyer and the philosophers who have interested themselves in anthropological records, would either pass by most of what are normally labelled as 'religious' practices, or place on the same level quite different phenomena.

THE COUNTER-INTUITIVE IS EVERYWHERE

Finally, in this chapter, I turn to another side of the problems raised by the Sperber and Boyer theory. If we were, for the sake of argument, to accept their characterization of the counter-intuitive and, like them, to identify religious-like phenomena with the counter-intuitive, this would seem to imply that the counter-intuitive, in their sense, is only, or mainly, to be found in certain specified areas of the sociocultural process that are rather exceptional, such as in religious phenomena.

Yet, if we turn again to the discussion concerning ancestors, and if we, once again, if only to a certain extent, follow the lead of Kopitoff when he argues for the identity of elders and ancestors, we realize that, if we were to label ancestors as counter-intuitive, we would justifiably have to do the same for elders or any other traditional office-holders. This is because behaviour toward elders, and indeed toward anybody for that matter, is far from straightforward. An elder is not treated as only the person in front of you, understood simply through the cognitive means which we all share as humans and which enable us to understand such phenomena as human intentionality but as an *elder,* that is, an entity which appears to be merely an old man, or sometimes an old woman, but is, in fact, endowed with a mysterious, non-empirical aura which means that they deserve respect. Furthermore, manifesting respect is, in many places in Africa, not merely politeness, since not to offer this respect will, through a mysterious unexplained causality, not of the conscious volition of the elder, cause disease, in exactly the same way as offended ancestors cause disease. Elders, therefore, must also be considered to be as much counter-intuitive as dead ancestors. Moreover, a moment's reflection will reveal that, although this is a particularly clear case, there is nothing special in this since the whole of social life involves behaving toward other human animals in terms of social roles and statuses. That is, in ways which are therefore informed by non-empirical, inferred characteristics which cannot possibly be directly derived from a hard-wired intuitive tool kit which we might possess for general understandings of the world and people. Thus, an element of the counter-intuitive, in the non-discursively marked sense of the term, is everywhere

Of course, an objection to the argument developed in the previous paragraph could be that, while ancestors are *only* counter-intuitive beings, elders are counter-intuitive beings and *also* intuitive beings. But this would be an awkward defence for a writer such as Boyer, since he insists that ancestors, too, are beings that can be understood intuitively apart from their little counter-intuitive extras. But the general point I am making in this chapter sweeps such questions aside for much more fundamental reasons. I argue that neither ancestors nor elders are normally perceived as counter-intuitive, since in ordinary circumstances their counter-intuitive potential is not cognitively salient because they are so familiar, while *sampy* and Christian 'beliefs' are protected from growing familiarity by a variety of devices such as the repetition of the phrase 'I believe'. This, of course, does not rule out the possibility that, in certain circumstances, *both* ancestors and elders may be temporarily realized as counter-intuitive in moments of metaphysical or political reflection, perhaps occasioned by the presence of an ethnographer.

I also accept, as noted earlier, that certain other phenomena can be (and, most of the time, are) given a counter-intuitive discursive prominence. This is the case with the *sampy*. A sign of this is that *sampy* are put in question and made a subject of talk, while the nature of ancestors usually is not. In other words, while the nature of ancestors and elders normally 'goes without saying' (see Bloch 1992), that *of sampy* and dragons does not. But this difference cuts across all kinds of phenomena, including religious-like phenomena, and therefore cannot be one of its distinctive features.

For example, studies on the understandings of kinship by Astuti (2001) and myself (see Bloch et al. 2001) have led the authors to argue that what is discursively salient concerning the transmission of characteristics between parents and children cannot be taken as expressing the principles of understanding of folk genetics among the persons studied, since these normally 'go without saying'. The basic principles of folk genetics are taken for granted, like the nature of ancestors, while the focused subjects of discourse are quite different, often counter-intuitive, in the sense that they add a further intriguing and challenging reflection to the unspoken general principles.

Thus, in a domain such as folk genetics we find the same mixture of occasionally evoked counter-intuitive elements and normally un-expressed intuitive assumptions as we find in what is, loosely and conventionally, called religion. The contrast between simpler beliefs and more reflexive beliefs which might be counter-intuitive is thus marked, not by the intrinsic character of the subject matter, whether genetics, ancestors, dragons or *sampy,* but by how it is treated and presented in certain discourses.

ACKNOWLEDGEMENTS

I would like to thank the following for important and constructive comments on earlier drafts of this chapter: R. Astuti, P. Boyer, N. Frankenberry, G. Lenclud, E. Keller, R. Rorty and D. Sperber.

NOTES

1. Turner gives ethnographic evidence that the statement about macaws is indeed to be taken in a way which could not be guessed out of context.
2. For a history of the *sampy*, see Dominichini 1985.
3. This corresponds exactly to the problem faced by the Christian missionaries in China discussed in Bell 2002.
4. Some new *sampy* have reappeared at times, like now, when Christianity seems to be failing many people.

REFERENCES

Astuti, R. 2001. 'Are We All Natural Dualists? A Developmental Cognitive Approach', *Journal of the Royal Anthropological Institute* n.s.(7): 429–47.

Bell, C. 2002. '"The Chinese Believe in Religion": Belief and Believing in the Study of Religion', in N. Frankenburg (ed.), *Radical Interpretation of Religion*, Cambridge: Cambridge University Press.

Bloch, M. 1986. *From Blessing to Violence*, Cambridge: Cambridge University Press.

——. 1992. 'What Goes Without Saying: The Conceptualisation of Zafimaniry Society', in A. Kuper (ed.), *Conceptualising Society*, London: Routledge.

Bloch, M., G. Solomon and S. Carey. 2001. 'Zafimaniry Understanding of What is Passed on from Parents to Children: A Cross-Cultural Approach', *Journal of Cognition and Culture* 1(1): 43–58.

Boyer, P. 1994. *The Naturalness of Religious Ideas*, Berkeley: University of California Press.

Crocker, C. 1985. 'My Brother the Parrot', in G. Urton (ed.), *Animal Myth and Metaphors in South America*, Salt Lake City: University of Utah Press.

Dominichini, J.-P. 1985. *Les Dieux au service des rois: histoire orale des Sampin' Andriana*, Paris: Editions du centre national de recherches scientifiques.

Evans-Pritchard, E. 1956. *Nuer Religion*, Oxford: Oxford University Press.

Fei Xiaotong. 1989. 'The World Without Ghosts', in R. Arkush and L. Lee (eds), *Land Without Ghosts*, Berkeley: University of California Press.

Kopitoff, I. 1971. 'Ancestors as Elders', *Africa* 41(11): 129–42.

Leach, E. 1954. *Political Systems of Highland Burma*, Cambridge MA: Harvard University Press.

Lenclud, G. 1990. 'Vues de l'esprit, art de l'autre', *Terrain* 14.

——. n.d. 'Beliefs, Culture and Reflexivity'. Unpublished manuscript.

Needham R. 1972. *Belief, Language and Experience*, Oxford: Blackwell.

Pouillon, J. 1979. 'Remarques sur le verbe "croire" ', in M. Izard and P. Smith (eds), *La Fonction symbolique*, Paris: Gallimard.

Sperber, D. 1982. 'Apparently Irrational Beliefs', in M. Hollis and S. Lukes (eds), *Rationality and Relativism*, Oxford: Blackwell.

—— . 1997. 'Intuitive and Reflexive Beliefs', *Mind and Language* 12(1): 67–83.

Thourangeau, R. and R. Sternberg. 1981. 'Aptness in Metaphor', *Cognitive Psychology* 13: 27–85.

CHAPTER 8

RITUAL AND DEFERENCE

Maurice Bloch

Anthropologists have been concerned with the puzzle caused by the observation that, while it is clear that rituals seem to be, in part at least, communicative acts – in that some kind of non-trivial information is conveyed and is involved for both participants and observers alike – it seems very difficult to be satisfactorily precise about what this content might be. It has even been suggested by many, including myself, that a precise decoding of the message of rituals is necessarily misleading (Bloch 1974; Sperber 1974; Lewis 1980; Humphrey and Laidlaw 1994). Some have gone so far as to argue that rituals are simply meaningless (Staal 1979), though exactly what such a claim would amount to is very unclear. However, one reason for arguing in this way is simply that, in the field, we are frustratingly and continually faced with informants who say that they don't know what rituals mean or why they are done in this or that way. Nonetheless, what stops anthropologists adhering easily to the thesis that rituals are meaningless is that these very same informants who a minute before admitted they did not know what elements of the ritual were about, add, at the same time, puzzlingly and portentously, that these elements mean something very deep and they insist that it is very important to perform them in precisely the right way.

In fact, anthropological discussions often suffer from the fact that they conflate the problem of writing the ethnography of ritual (symbolic analysis) and the problem of understanding the meaning of what is going on for the participants. But leaving this point aside, anthropologists nevertheless often leave us with the rather lame point that rituals convey something or other that is vague but somehow powerful. Here I want to follow a tradition in ritual analysis that, instead of being embarrassed about vagueness, makes it its central concern. This is what I want to be precise about. Furthermore, I want to go much beyond my predecessors, myself included, in arguing that the vagueness of ritual offers us a clue to the nature of much human social knowledge and of many learning processes.

REPETITION

One feature which has often been noted in discussions concerning ritual is the presence of repetition (Leach 1966; Bloch 1974; Rappaport 1975; Lewis 1980). In fact, the term 'repetition' in these discussions is used to refer to quite a variety of phenomena, all of which are commonly present in rituals.

First of all, the same elements or phrases are often repeated in the same performance, sometimes to a bewildering extent. For example, in a type of Malagasy circumcision ritual the same phrase can recur several hundred times, perhaps even more; similarly, in Christian rituals the word 'Amen' is also said many times. Secondly, there is the fact that whole rituals are often repetitions one of another. One weekly Mass is in many parts much the same as that of the week before. Finally, actors in rituals guide much of their behaviour in terms of what they believe others, or themselves, to have done or said on previous occasions. In this sense they are repeating either themselves or others. Indeed, any act, whether a speech act or otherwise, that appears to originate fully with the actor cannot properly be called a ritual in English.

It is repetition of this latter type that I want to concentrate on. At least some, if not most, of the actions involved in some kinds of phenomena are understood, by actors and observers alike, as repetitions; that is, they are acts, whether speech acts or acts of another kind, that do not completely originate in the intentionality of the producer at the time of his or her performance. This point is most important and, with the notable exceptions of Humphrey and Laidlaw (1994) and Keane (1997), whose arguments are somewhat similar to mine, has not been stressed enough in the literature. It means that what is involved in ritual is conscious 'repetition', either of oneself or, much more often and much more importantly, of others whom one has seen or heard perform the ritual before. All rituals thus involve what can be called 'quotation', if we use the term to refer not just to language, but to all repetitions of originators. These originators must have some sort of authority, and this authority justifies quoting them, as in the Lord's Prayer or the Christian communion service.

Familiar statements given to anthropologists by participants in rituals, such as 'We do this because it is the custom of the ancestors', 'We do this because it is what one does at these events', or 'We do this because we have been ordered to act in this way', imply conscious quotation.

Therefore, the inevitable implication of such statements is that, for both participants and onlookers, it is not just the specific present context of time and place that frames the intentionality of the acts of the ritual actor and that is relevant to fully understanding them, but also the past time and space context of specified, or unspecified, previous occurrences of the repeated/quoted acts. As Humphrey and Laidlaw put it, in a way that echoes a point I made in an earlier article (Bloch 1974), 'ritualization transforms the relation between intention and the meaning of action' (Humphrey and Laidlaw 1994: 90).

When a Malagasy, during a circumcision ceremony, sprays water by way of blessing on those present, everyone knows that he or she is doing this kind of action in this way because this is 'what one does', that is, the tradition. This means that whatever the elder feels like at the time, and the way he perceives the situation, will be insufficient to explain, and is well known to be insufficient to explain, why he is using water at that moment. Compare this with a situation wherein he was merely reaching for water from a stream; in this case most observers would find it sufficient, not necessarily rightly, that, given his background knowledge, the twin facts that the person was thirsty and that he saw the water in front of him – that is, his beliefs and desires, in the psychological/philosophical sense of the terms – was all there was to it.

The fact that rituals involve, and are known by everyone concerned to involve, quotation, in the broad sense in which I have been using the word, is not all there is to a phenomenon such as a Malagasy blessing; but it is surely a highly significant part of it. In what follows I turn to an examination of what this fact might imply, given the centrality that has been accorded to the reading of the intentionality of speakers for semantics in general and for linguistic utterances in particular.

DEFERENCE, UNDERSTANDING AND TRUTH

Rituals therefore are acts of repetition or quotation. Such a remark places ritual within what externalist philosophers have identified as a central aspect of human thought and communication (Putman 1975) and which has been called by some 'deference' (Burge 1986), that is, reliance on the authority of others to guarantee the value of what is said or done. What makes such an observation particularly interesting for anthropologists is that deference fundamentally alters the relation between understanding and holding something to be true. It seems common sense that to hold something to be true one must also understand it. This, however, is not the case when deference is involved, especially when deference is linked to quotation.

Roughly, we can say that, in pragmatic theories of the Gricean family type (Grice 1971; Sperber and Wilson 1986), understanding meaning is seen to necessarily require not only knowledge of the lexicon and of the syntax employed, but also the unconscious reading of the mind of the speaker and of what she intends as she utters the sounds. Without such 'mind reading' the words are, at the very least, so open to a wide range of ambiguities that it is impossible for the hearer to process them successfully. Such a theory is all the more interesting in that it makes the understanding of language depend directly on what many would now argue is *the* key distinguishing feature of *Homo sapiens sapiens,* the so-called theory of mind, which enables a person to 'read' the mind of others and which separates mankind fairly sharply from all other animal species (Premack 1991).

Quotation implies an obvious modification of the simple Gricean principles considered above. It throws the hearer back to trying to read not only the mind of the speaker, but also the mind of the speaker who is being quoted. Given the metarepresentational ability of human beings, this is easily done, even if we are dealing with further degrees of metarepresentation (Sperber 2000). In this case, once the quoted sentence is understood, its truth or otherwise can be considered.

Quotation, however, offers another possibility. This is a kind of abandonment of the examination of the truth of the quoted statement, because one is only concerned with the fact that the statement has been made and that the speaker has been identified. If this speaker is worthy of trust, one can assume that what has been said is true without making the effort of understanding. In such a case deference is combined with quotation, and it accounts for the rather odd possibility that one may hold something to be true without fully understanding it. If one trusts the source sufficiently, understanding is not necessary for the truth to be accepted, as is illustrated by the following example given by Origgi (2000). She tells us of a follower who is convinced of the truth of a statement made by a leader who asserted that there are too many neo-Trotskyites in their party, even though she knows that she has no idea what a neo-Trotskyite might be. She will then be happy to transmit the information to another without understanding it. This might seem an unusual scenario, but a moment's reflection will confirm that we are all, to varying degrees, in much this same sort of situation, most of the time.

DEFERENCE AND SOCIAL LIFE

What is particularly interesting for anthropologists in an example such as the one just given is that not only do such occurrences crop up continually but that their occurrence is not random in the course of social life. Situations when the truth of certain propositions is to be accepted through deference, and therefore not necessarily understood, are socially and culturally organized and regulated. Living in a partially institutionalized form of life, which is what is meant by living in society, means that there are moments, concepts and contexts the why and wherefores of which one may examine and moments, concepts and contexts where this is inappropriate. For the reason we have seen above, this means that the latter need not be understood.

Thus, social life 'manages', so to speak, the occurrence and the nature of deference through different types of institutional devices and therefore, at the same time, it establishes an economy of the necessity of understanding. It is clear that living in a socially organized system, even the apparently most *ad hoc*, nonetheless involves moments of compulsory deference, in the sense used above. There are moments when there are not only limits to understanding, but limits to the appropriateness of attempting to understand. The ordinary continual deference of practical life does not simply involve delaying our search for intentionality, but often apparently largely *abandoning* it. This means that all normal human communication involves a mixture of searching for meaning, our own and that of others, and *also* not searching, moments of understanding and not understanding. When young children exhaust their parents by endlessly asking 'why' questions, they may well be training their judgement of when to search and when not to search. Consider the example of someone who tells us that the cat is on the mat; in such a circumstance we may well search for the reason why they want to inform us of this fact, but we would be very unwise to waste our time searching for the reason why they chose that particular sound to convey the concept 'car'.

We have seen why deference makes holding something true without understanding it possible, but there is also a reason why social life makes this abandonment of the search for meaning common. The reason is that the experience of living in a historically constructed system means that deference continually occurs without the individual who is being deferred to being easily identifiable. As a result, intentionality cannot be 'locked' on to an intending mind and therefore understanding cannot be 'clinched'. People around us and ourselves are clearly deferring to others. But if we were so unwise as to want to examine these others more closely, they would turn out to be deferring to yet others, and so on, without the process having any clear boundary. This is because humans live and act within a set of conventions, which are no doubt the product of a long historical process of communication and quotation, and which are experienced as 'given', that is, without specific minds intending them. These are the conventions that have been so internalized as to be completely unconscious. Anthropologists sometimes call them culture or habitus and sometimes give them other names such as structure. In other words we are continually deferring to others, but we do not catch sight of the minds we are deferring to. For we are not simply reading human minds, we are reading historically constructed human minds. We do not simply understand others and ourselves; we always, to varying degrees, but semi-consciously, understand that people around us are deferring to invisible and indeterminable others and that therefore we should limit our attempt to understand them. What this means is that complete understanding is impossible because, as noted above, full understanding requires that, either immediately or at one or more remove, as in quotation, it is in the end possible to imagine the intentionality of some mind or other. But, if it is not possible to identify clearly an original intentional being, meaning can never be grasped.

Of course, such indeterminate deference is much of the time unconscious, but this is certainly not always the case. The case of the follower
accepting the belief about the neo-Trotskyites is a case where it is quite
possible that the act of deference becomes conscious, although, there, the
person deferred to is clearly identified. What difference this consciousness of deference makes has not been, as far as I know, much explored
in pragmatics, or in philosophy, but since it is so prominent in ritual and
religion and so closely linked with the question of exegesis, we will have
to consider the question.

There are therefore three elements in human communication that can
be combined: (1) quotation and deference, (2) consciousness of deference, (3) lack of clarity as to who is being deferred to. When all three
are present, we have the phenomena that in anthropological English are
commonly referred to as ritual. Because the combination of these three
elements is likely to lead to limited understanding, it is not surprising
that this state of affairs is frequent in ritual.

DEFERENCE AND RELIGION

Now we have the tools to examine what all this might mean for ritual and
religion. At first, I examine two apparently simple deference scenarios,
both of which correspond quite closely to the Origgi story about the neo-
Trotskyites. The first concerns learning the Koran in Muslim schools,
and the second concerns spirit possession.

Reading or reciting the Koran, which is the central purpose of Muslim
education, apparently involves a simple type of quotation on the part of
the student since the speaker is merely quoting a single other intentional
mind: that of God, to whom he defers totally (Eickelman 1978). The
student should, ideally, learn the Koran perfectly by heart and so become
a totally transparent medium just like Muhammad himself. He should
become a sort of tape recorder, so that his intentionality, and thus his
understanding, disappear or become irrelevant to the text. As a result,
the speaker or the hearer can focus entirely on the presence of God in the
words. The student should efface himself as much as possible.

Another example of such ideally 'transparent' quotation is spirit possession. Theoretically, the utterer of sound has totally surrendered her
body, and especially her vocal organs, to the being who temporally pos-
sesses her. In this case too, the locus of emission of the sound should

ideally disappear. Asking the student of the Koran, or the medium, to explain her choice of words or content – that is, to provide an exegesis – would clearly be to deny her complete deference.

These two examples may seem simple, but in fact they involve two quite different elements. The student learning the Koran, and others around him, believe that what is proposed there is true and they must assert it whether they understand it or not. The medium has so effaced herself that the assertions that come from her mouth must be true, because the spiritual source speaks irrespective of her understanding. This is straightforward. However, one might expect that such practices might simply place at one remove the effort to understand. Having got the student or the medium out of the way, it should be possible to concentrate on understanding God or the spirit. This, however, does not seem to be the case. In such practices the act of deference takes centre stage and everybody joins with the student or the medium in abandoning their intentionality and in making themselves transparent to whoever's words they are quoting, which strangely fade out of focus.

The medium or the student is implicitly claiming truth for his utterance at very time that he is denying the relevance of his understanding what he is saying. The devout Muslim aligns him- or herself with the position of the student and therefore accepts the deference. It seems probable that the spectator at a séance never imagines a direct relation with the spirit but always a relation *via* the medium, in which case the deference comes into play also, probably because of the drama of self-attack. The effort in being transparent, that is, in deferring totally, is the real focus of the action.

In such cases we have two of the elements isolated above: deference and the consciousness of deference, even though this may ultimately disappear. What is not present, however, is the third element discussed above: the indetermination of the originating mind. It is clear that it is God who is the source of the Koran or it is Great-Grandmother who is the spirit. But what happens when such definition disappears? It is to this that I now turn.

RITUAL

It is the presence of the third element that characterizes much ritual and, more especially, those ritual elements that are most strongly resistant to exegesis. In such instances quotation, and therefore deference, is obviously taking place, but it is not clear who is being quoted or deferred to.

As noted above, a very common experience among anthropologists who ask why someone is doing something in a particular way in a ritual is to be answered by such phrases as 'It's the tradition', 'It is the custom of the ancestors', 'It goes back to early history', and so on. Now, these apparently frustrating answers are nonetheless interesting in many ways, for they combine explicitness concerning deference and awareness of imprecision about who exactly is the originating mind behind the practice.

The reference to tradition, or the ways in which things have always been done, or to the ancestors, clearly does throw the attention of the participants *away* from the intentionality of the actor but *to where in particular* is not so clear. Sperber, in a famous earlier paper, gave an example of this sort of thing when talking of a man who had asked him to shoot a dragon. He, quite rightly, stressed that we should bear in mind the quotational character of such a request. The man was not fully committed to the existence of dragons but was quoting others whose minds were questionable (Sperber 1982). This situation seems to me different from rituals. Rituals are even vaguer as to who the individual mind originating the message might be. Scrutiny of the source of the authority inevitably leads the inquirer into an endless regress. Thus, although we normally think of tradition as something being handed forward from the past to the present, the appeal to the *authority* of tradition, something that is socially much more central, involves being handed back from the present toward an indeterminable past destination.

If we imagine the participants, or the observers, in such rituals as the Mass, or the Malagasy initiation ritual, or making the sign of the cross, trying to work out who intended what they are doing to be done so, in other words trying for exegesis, they are going to be in a difficult situation.

Exegesis, that is, the search for original intentionality, is in itself perfectly reasonable, and although frustrating, almost inevitable. After all, we are dealing with people with human minds, that is, with animals whose minds are characterized by an intentionality-seeking device that is normally exercised ceaselessly, one might almost say obsessively, sometimes consciously but often unconsciously, and that enables them to read the minds of others and thus coordinate their behaviour with them. But in a ritual, these poor little animals, among them poor little anthropologists, appear to be faced with an impossible situation because the search for intentionality leads them ever further back, to ever more remote authorities, but without ever settling anywhere with any finality. This is the predicament of participants who might unwisely ask themselves why on earth they are doing this or that, as well as that of mere onlookers asking the same question.

This Kafkaesque nightmare of being endlessly referred back to other authorities can only be rendered bearable in one of three ways:

1. The first is the most straightforward. One can attempt to simply switch off the intentionality-seeking device, an attitude which could be described as retreat or 'putting on hold' or 'letting things be'. This switching-off requires some effort as, given the way our minds work, it is unnatural, but it can be done nonetheless. Saying that what you do, or what you say, is because of 'tradition' may in some cases be nothing more than an expression of this attitude. The refusal to look for intentionality, however, presents the participants with a disappointing propositional thinness. It is doubtful whether it is at all possible to entertain any relevant propositional content without placing it within the framework of propositional attitudes. And it is obvious that one cannot detect propositional attitudes without imagining a mind to which these attitudes belong. It is as if, when we are very tired and kept awake by a hubbub of voices, we apparently make out somebody or other saying, 'Raindrops are Jesus macaroons.' In such a situation, we might make no effort to discover the intentionality of the speaker and hope to go back to sleep as quickly as possible. My early memory of Catholic rituals is of this sort. It is probably accurate to say that such a proposition, totally devoid of attributable intentionality, has no meaning, or at least no utterer meaning, to use a Gricean distinction. The only thing we have got from it is the realization that it involves the use of proper language, therefore that it probably has potential for utterer meaning. Clearly there is here no understanding, and it is far from clear whether anybody in such a situation even holds the propositions to be true.

2. The second possibility is much more common but will also appear in a number of somewhat exceptional situations, being faced by an overly

inquisitive anthropologist being one, but not the only one. Then, for some reason, it will seem necessary to make an effort to understand what is going on. At first, one is tempted to search in the dark recesses behind the producer of the ritual acts, who after all we know is only quoting someone, somewhere, who might have meant to mean something. (Doing this without paying attention to informants is called functionalism in anthropology.) But it's dark behind there, for, as soon as persons seem to come into focus, they become transparent as they reveal other persons behind them. They are only deferring to someone else, further back, who, when focused upon, becomes similarly transparent, and so on. Finally, we give up searching for meaning, though not in the same total way as the giving up I discussed in case 1 and for the following reason.

All this frustration only occurs over the problem of searching for the intentionality of the initiator of the message. By contrast, the intentionality of the speaker, the singer or the actor in the ritual is not more problematic than those of the spirit medium or of the student learning the Koran who were discussed earlier. The intentionality of all these people can simply be read as deferential, and this act is greatly valued. The search for intentionality is therefore switched to the unproblematic examination of the intentionality of the transmitter, the situation that Humphrey and Laidlaw describe for the Jain *Puja* (Humphrey and Laidlaw 1994). And when people tell us that they don't know what such a phrase means, or why such an act is performed, but that it is being said or performed in this way because one is following the customs of the ancestors, they are surely telling us that what they are doing, saying, singing, is above all *deferring*. In such a case there is no exegesis to be expected from the participants, and it is indeed offensive to ask for it, as this denies what they are doing. The reason they do not understand the content of what they are doing is that its originators cannot be localized as intentional minds, and no speaker meaning can thus be attributed to them. However, this indeterminacy does not eliminate the authority behind the content, an authority that claims truth for it. It is this situation that so puzzles the decoding anthropologists, but that is exactly what is analysed by Burge: that is, claiming truth for what one does not understand. This situation is simply muddled by traditional worries about the presence or absence of exegesis, though it is possible that, in such a case, the people involved will accept that exegesis from somebody else is possible and that experts, somewhere or other, know the 'meaning' of what is going on.

3. It is possible, however, that even this solution to the problem is un-satisfactory. In rare but important moments, people are going to ask themselves, or others, why things are done or said in this or that way, and they will not give up in spite of the apparent difficulties encountered in their search. Their mind-reading instinct will just not leave them alone. Thus, one wants to attribute speaker meaning to what is going on but in order to do that one must inevitably create some sort of speaker. Normal speakers are not available since these will become transparent as soon as they are considered and will therefore perform the disappearing act discussed above. Again, this situation is identical whether we are dealing with frequently or rarely occurring rituals, since participants may wonder about the meaning of an action such as crossing oneself, or seeing others cross themselves, as rarely, or as frequently, as they might about the meaning of a plant in a New Guinea initiation ritual.

The solution to the problem of wanting to locate meaning without having normal originators to that meaning is to merge all the shadowy transparent figures into a phantasmagorical quasi-person who may be called something like 'tradition', 'the ancestors as a group', 'our way of doing things', 'our spirit', 'our religion', even perhaps 'God'. These are entities to which 'minds' may just about be attributed with some degree of plausibility, thus apparently restoring intentional meaning to the goings-on of ritual. The apparent specificity of such entities thus appears, at first, to solve the problem of the indeterminacy of the intentional source. After all, we are familiar with the attribution of human-like intentional minds to things like mountains, or dead people (Boyer 1996), so why not to an essentialized tradition? There we are in a situation that is somewhat similar and somewhat dissimilar to that of 2. It is similar in that the message is held to be true whether it is understood or not. Again, the act of deference is consciously present and valued in and of itself. However, the act of deference does not hold centre stage as much as in 2, because speaker meaning becomes an alternative point of interest. Nonetheless, this is no ordinary speaker meaning to the extent that the 'speaker' is no ordinary mind, the kind of mind we instinctively know how to interpret with great subtlety because of our probably innate 'theory of mind'. In fact, I would propose that the precision of our understanding varies with the degree that the phantasmagoric initiators are close or distant to ordinary minds. Thus, the mind of an entity called 'the tradition' would be more difficult to interpret than that of an entity called 'the ancestors', but that is, in turn, probably more difficult to interpret than a singular spirit, simply because the concept of plural minds is not what we are equipped to understand. The difficulties of exegesis in such cases should thus correlate with the degree of the normal, human-like characteristics of the entities who halt the endless regress caused by deference.

The three variants discussed above are of course not distinct in time or place. Individuals may slide from one to another during a particular ritual. However, the form of the ritual and the entities invoked will ensure the general organization in most people's minds of relative degrees of understanding. This is because the problems of attributing clear meanings to what is done all result from the central fact that ritual involves high degrees of deference. This emphasis actually fits well with the quite different type of discussion of ritual I developed in *Prey into Hunter* (Bloch 1992), where I argue that the first element of ritual is a kind of dramatized self-attack by participants, an attack against their own intentionality, so that it may be replaced. What I identified as the preliminary violence in ritual (for example: the weakening of the sacrificial animal, which stands for the humans involved) can be seen as the theatre of deference. Rituals are moments when the actors make themselves transparent so that other intentional minds can be read through them. Once again what characterizes ritual is conscious deference.

However, as we have seen, deference is a common aspect of human life. It occurs whenever we do something, or believe something to be true, relying on the authority of others, something that we do constantly. If people are always partly, but very significantly, living in a sea of deference, this is largely an unconscious fact. But nevertheless, it is a fact that hovers not very far from the level of consciousness, and that can, and often does, cross into the level of consciousness. As Putman (1975) stressed, people are almost conscious of the fact that they are constantly relying on the understanding of others and that they normally act in terms of beliefs they do not fully understand, but which they hold valid because of their trust in the understanding of others. This is also the situation described by Hutchins, which he defines as 'distributed cognition' (1995). People therefore allow themselves to depend on others. By and large, this is a good feeling, while at other times it is oppressive. But, when one is in trouble, and one does not know what to do, one allows oneself to be taken over by the knowledge and the authority of others; it is only sensible, and there is nothing much else that one can do.

Now I am arguing that ritual is just that – in a rather extreme form, rituals are orgies of conscious deference. But if this is so, the search for exegesis is always misleading. This is not because it is impossible. Clearly exegeses exist, whether private or shared, whether the secret of experts or available to all, whether conscious, semi-conscious, or unconscious. But they are beside the point of the central character of ritual: deference.

REFERENCES

Bloch, M. 1974. 'Symbols, Song, Dance and Features of Articulation or Is Religion an Extreme Form of Traditional Authority?', *Archives Européenes de Sociologie* 5: 55–81.

——. 1986. *From Blessing to Violence: History and Ideology in the Circumcision Ritual of the Merina of Madagascar*, Cambridge: Cambridge University Press.

——. 1991. 'Language, Anthropology and Cognitive Science', *Man* 26: 183–98.

——. 1992. *Prey into Hunter: The Politics of Religious Experience*, Cambridge: Cambridge University Press.

Boyer, P. 1996. 'What Makes Anthropomorphism Natural: Intuitive Ontology and Cultural Representations', *Journal of the Royal Anthropological Institute* 2: 83–98.

Burge,T. 1986. 'Individualism and Psychology', *Philosophical Review* 95: 133–201.

Eickelman, D. 1978. 'The Art of Memory: Islamic Education and Social Reproduction', *Comparative Studies in Society and History* 20: 485–516.

Grice, H. 1971. 'Utterer's Meaning, Sentence Meaning and Word Meaning', in J. Searle (ed.), *The Philosophy of Language*, Oxford: Oxford University Press.

Humphrey, C. and J. Laidlaw. 1994. *The Archetypal Actions of Ritual*, Oxford: Oxford University Press.

Hutchins, E. 1995. *Cognition in the Wild*, Cambridge, MA: MIT Press.

Keane, W. 1997. *Signs of Recognition*, Berkeley: University of California Press.

Leach, E. 1966. 'Ritualisation in Man in Relation to Conceptual and Social Development', *Philosophical Transactions of the Royal Society* 251: 403–8.

Lewis, G. 1980. *Day of Shining Red*, Cambridge: Cambridge University Press.

Origgi, G. 2000. 'Croire sans Comprendre', *Cahiers de Philosophie de L'Université de Caen* 34: 191–202.

Premack, D. 1991. 'Does the Chimpanzee Have a Theory of Mind? Revisited', in R. Byrne and A. Whitten (eds), *Machiavellian Intelligence*, Oxford: Oxford University Press.

Putman, H. 1975. 'The Meaning of "Meaning"', in K. Gunderson (ed.), *Language, Mind and Knowledge*, Minneapolis: University of Minnesota Press.

Rappaport, R. 1975. 'The Obvious Aspects of Ritual', *Cambridge Anthropology* 2: 3–61.

Sperber, D. 1974. *Le Symbolisme en général*, Paris: Hermann.

——. 1982. *Le Savoir des anthropologues*, Paris: Hermann.

—— (ed.). 2000. *Metarepresentations: A Multidisciplinary Perspective*, Oxford: Oxford University Press.

Sperber, D. and D. Wilson. 1986. *Relevance: Communication and Cognition*, Oxford: Blackwell.

Staal, F. 1979. 'The Meaninglessness of Ritual', *Numen* 26: 2–22.

Whitehouse, H. 2002. 'Religious Reflexivity and Transmissive Frequency', *Social Anthropology* 10: 91–103

CHAPTER 9

KINSHIP AND EVOLVED PSYCHOLOGICAL DISPOSITIONS

THE MOTHER'S-BROTHER CONTROVERSY RECONSIDERED[1]

Maurice Bloch and Dan Sperber

One of the most discussed topics in the history of anthropology has been the significance of the relationship between mother's brother and sister's son in patrilineal societies. However, the subject seems to have entirely faded from the hot topics of the discipline since the 1960s. We believe that, in reviewing this academic story of strange excitement and then total neglect, we can both understand some of the fundamental epistemological problems of anthropology and suggest some of the ways in which new approaches might throw light on questions which have tended to be abandoned rather than resolved.

THE HISTORY OF THE MOTHER'S-BROTHER CONTROVERSY

The behaviour which so intrigued anthropologists involved the rights, recognized in many unrelated patrilineal societies, of a male member of the junior generation over the property and even the persons and wives of senior male members of his mother's lineage, typically the mother's brother.[2] The example which came to be most discussed was that of the BaThonga of Southern Africa because of the particularly full and surprising description of the customs involved given by the early missionary ethnographer Henri Junod in 1912. There the relation primarily concerned the right of mutual insult between the sister's son and the mother's brother and his wives and unclear claims to the property of the mother's brother by the sister's son. The tolerated violence of the behaviour, as well as its sexual overtones, contributed to the fascination with the custom and probably titillated the various scholars who discussed the subject. But it was not so much this one example which interested scholars as the conviction that they were dealing with a peculiar relationship which occurred again and again in many totally unrelated societies, something which was all the more unexpected in that it contradicted patrilineal organizational principles – since a mother's brothers and sister's sons must usually belong to different lineages – and the respect usually accorded to senior generations.

Examples of this peculiar relationship were thought to have been found among Australian Aborigines and in Amazonia, southern Europe, Oceania and India, not to mention other parts of Africa. Even today recent ethnographers have been struck, again and again, by the prominence accorded to this relationship by the people they have studied in many different places, for example, northern India (Jamous 1991), Amazonia (Viveiros de Castro 1992), and Melanesia (Gillison 1993). But this apparent recurrence itself raises a problem. The various manifestations which so many anthropologists have recognized as instances of the peculiar mother's-brother/sister's-son relationship are clearly cognate. At the same time, these cases turn out, on closer examination, to be very varied – sometimes involving symmetrical joking, sometimes asymmetrical joking, sometimes avoidance, sometimes significant economic privileges, sometimes sexual rights, sometimes only ritual manifestations – and, furthermore, while in some cases it is actual mother's brothers and sister's sons who have the rights in question, the relation sometimes involves broad classificatory groups. The variation is in fact so great that it becomes very difficult to say exactly what it is that the various examples share, and this inevitably has made many wonder whether the scholars who have turned their attention to the question have not been dealing with a nonexistent category.

At first, anthropologists assuming a universal history for humankind along a single evolutionary path and, implicitly, a universal cognitive representation of filiation and marriage saw in such practices as the aggressive claim of the sister's son to his mother's brother's property a survival of mother right and proof of the existence of an earlier matrilineal stage (Rivers 1924). This explanation was then famously dismissed by Radcliffe-Brown (1924), who, using his refutation to demonstrate the character of structural-functional accounts, supplied a synchronic explanation for the practice. Thus the controversy over the mother's brother could not have been more central to the short history of social anthropological theory, and the success of Radcliffe-Brown's argument was a key element in the gradual marginalization of notions of evolution from the mainstream of the discipline.

Radcliffe-Brown's explanation was, at first, mainly in terms of the extension of sentiment. He argued that the sentiments of a child toward its mother were extended to the mother's family, making the mother's brother a kind of male mother who acted accordingly in a maternal fashion and so gave gifts to his sister's son. More important, however, was the argument that such customs could only be understood in terms of their function as part of the total social structure. Radcliffe-Brown's argument therefore not only went against evolutionism but also was to be a dramatic demonstration of the value of what has come to be known as structural-functionalism. For Radcliffe-Brown, therefore, the idea of an identical and single history of humankind was to be abandoned, but a universalistic element remained in that he assumed a universal cognitive basis for the representation of kinship; mothers were always mothers, and patriliny's attempt to underplay this caused problems which had to be resolved by strange customs. Furthermore, because of the commonality of the fundamental building blocks of kinship systems, large-scale comparisons could be made between societies, which were to be the foundations of the new 'natural science of society'.

In turn, Radcliffe-Brown was criticized by Fortes (1953) and then by Goody (1959), who, while retaining the fundamental principle of a synchronic explanation in terms of a systematic social structure, criticized Radcliffe-Brown's explanation for being over-general, since it would predict a much greater degree of universality and uniformity than the evidence warranted. Goody's criticism took the form of noting that, although the sentiments of children toward their mothers were everywhere the same, the specific practice in question was found only in certain societies that had patrilineal descent groups without the counterbalance of matrilineal inheritance and that any explanation had to be tied to the occurrence of this type of group. Furthermore, and here following the later Radcliffe-Brown, he specified the character of the institution much more narrowly than the earlier evolutionist writers, insisting on the element of privileged aggression in the snatching of property by the sister's son in ritual contexts. This strange custom he explained, as did Fortes, in terms of the contradiction between what he argued was a universally bilateral kinship system and the occasionally occurring unilineal descent system. He argued that sister's sons were grandchildren of their mother's fathers in the kinship system and therefore their heirs, while in the descent system they were in no way their successors, since descent was traced only in the patrilineal line. The tolerated snatching of meat by the sister's son at his mother's brother's sacrifices resolved this contradiction because in this way he recovered some of his grandparental inheritance from the son of his maternal grandparents, who had (abusively in terms of the kinship system but legitimately in terms of the descent system) received all of that inheritance. Goody clinched this argument with a comparison of two closely related groups with different property systems in which the degree of inheritance 'deprivation' of the sister's son was correlated with the importance of meat-snatching.

This piece of work is a particularly fine example of the structural-functional analyses of its time. It assumes, with a characteristically confident tone, that comparison of the social structures of different societies will reveal recurring connections between different features which, it can then be assumed, are related in a synchronic causal way. This sort of comparison also implies a belief that the basic institutions of societies are everywhere of much the same kind, that they are represented in much the same way, and that we know that all human societies have men and women, marriage, and filiation. According to this way of thinking, patriliny is a particular perspective imposed on the universally recognized facts of procreation. The belief in the universality of the basic representations of kinship of Radcliffe-Brown is thus modified but not abandoned, since these representations, when they occur, are about natural, objective facts that exist independently. Furthermore, the emotional reaction to a certain state of affairs, in this case ambiguity over filiation, is assumed to be basically the same for all humans irrespective of culture and to produce, therefore, similar behaviours in similar circumstances. These different but related assumptions of a common ground are what made the use of comparison as a discovery procedure possible. Variations were significant because it could be assumed that they occurred within the same natural field consisting of identifiable elements; thus the general principles of Radcliffe-Brown's natural comparative science of society remained possible.

This identity of the basic building blocks of kinship systems is precisely what came under challenge in the subsequent development of the discipline. The first clearly expressed formulation of the coming epistemological shift is to be found in Leach's 1955 paper on marriage, and this shift was emphatically repeated and expanded in Needham's introduction to *Rethinking Kinship and Marriage* (1971). The basis of their arguments was that marriage and kinship, as understood by social and cultural anthropologists, were not externally existing phenomena but merely glosses for loosely similar notions found in different cultures. As Needham put it, there was no such *thing* as kinship. Subsequently, in a more empirical mood, Schneider (1984) attempted to demonstrate that Austronesian kinship was a fundamentally different phenomenon from European kinship and therefore aiming at understanding the former with the words appropriate for the latter was a source of confusion. Thus, generalizing comparisons of kinship systems were impossible because they did not, as was previously assumed, involve comparisons of like with like.

Similar in inspiration but even more startling – though to many less convincing in its extreme forms – was the point made by a number of feminists that there were no such things as women and men beyond a specific cultural context. Explicitly drawing on Schneider's critique of kinship, Collier and Yanagisako (1987) argued that the differentiation between female and male that anthropologists had incorporated into their analyses was a 'cultural construction' and of a quite different order from any sexual difference between organisms that might exist in nature. These anti-naive-empiricist points had two consequences for the kind of argument that Radcliffe-Brown, Fortes and Goody had presented. First of all, as was noted above, it could be argued that the grand comparisons of structural-functionalism involved operations such as adding apples and pears, and, secondly, the social units, for example lineages, were not similar 'natural things' occurring in different societies but different and unique historical/cultural representations constructed in different settings and therefore incommensurable (see Kuper 1982). The only reason, according to these writers, that kinship had seemed so similar among different human groups across the globe was an ethnocentric tendency to see similarities and overlook differences. Finally, the last universalistic element in the Goody argument, the similarity of behavioural response in all humans to similar situations, also came under attack by anthropologists who claimed that emotions too were culturally constructed (Rosaldo 1980) and could therefore not be intuited from introspective sympathy.

The implication of all this for the type of comparative enterprise that Goody and others had been engaged in seemed clear: it made it impossible. It led, if not necessarily at least quite directly, to the deep relativism of much modern anthropology. The systematic comparison, which for the structural-functionalists was to be a first step toward scientific generalizations, became clearly illegitimate if there could be no assurance that the units of analyses were commensurate. Those who studied kinship had deluded themselves that they had been dealing with biological facts, which it would be reasonable to assume would be severely constrained by nature and therefore comparable, while in reality they had been dealing with representations which, it was implicitly assumed, were the product of unique histories and therefore could take any form at all. In the case of the particular example of the mother's-brother controversy, the recurrence of the institution which had intrigued the earlier writers was a mirage. Every case was different, and the very terms of the relationship – mother, brother, sister and son – did not indicate the same kind of thing in different cultural contexts. Thus, just as structural-functionalism had dealt the first blow to anthropology as a natural science, the culturalist attack on structural-functionalism seemed to have destroyed any hope of generalization. We had been left with nothing but anecdotes about the infinity of specific situations in which human beings find themselves.

The theoretical history we have just traced can be seen as unidirectional; it is the history of the gradual abandonment of belief in the possibility of anthropology as a generalizing science. It assumes that because human beings can transmit information between individuals through symbolic communication they are entirely free of any natural constraints and essentially different from other animals, who transmit most, if not all, information genetically. Animals must wait for changes in their genomes to become different; humans, in contrast, change with their representations. The existence of these representations is made possible by the learning and computational potential of the human brain, but their contents, it is implicitly assumed, are not *at all* constrained or even influenced by genetically inherited brain 'hardware'. These contents are determined, rather, by historico-cultural processes. Human history is therefore liberated from biology, and people may represent the world and each other as they please. The belief in the need for cross-cultural regularities resisting historical specificity becomes simply wrong, the product of a category mistake. The extension of the aims of natural science to the study of culture and society would be like studying smells with rulers.

The aim of this chapter is not to deny the validity of at least some of the criticisms of earlier anthropological approaches which have just been touched on. Indeed, we recognize the relevance of those arguments, and there is no doubt that the whole enterprise of Radcliffe-Brownian structural-functional analysis rested in part on the dubious foundations of misplaced naive realism. We agree with Leach, Needham and Schneider that the phenomena described by anthropologists under the label of 'kinship' are cultural and therefore historical constructions and that people's thoughts and actions are about these constructions rather than about unmediated facts of biological kinship. The implicit argument which would see representations of kinship, marriage and gender as merely the inevitable recognition of 'the way things are' will not do. We will argue, however, that this does not mean that the attempt to invoke natural factors or even biological factors as explanations of such cultural representations must be abandoned as though these representations and the people who hold them had somehow floated free from the earth into the immaterial clouds of history. Antirealism too can be utterly naive.

We choose the example of the mother's-brother/sister's-son relationship in patrilineal societies to demonstrate our argument simply because it has been so critical in the history of the discipline, and we try to show that it is possible to envisage, in a case such as this, an approach which combines the particular with the general, although we must recognize that the actual carrying out of such a study lies beyond what we can do here.

The abandonment of overpowerful theories in anthropology came, in the first place, from the realization that the implicit and explicit cultural 'universals' of traditional anthropology were not as uniform as they had been assumed to be. But anthropologists who argue for a radically relativistic constructivism often seem to lack confidence in their own arguments. Their reasoning has taken them to a point that negates what all those with a reasonable acquaintance with the ethnographic record know – which is that the regularities which have fascinated the discipline since its inception are surprisingly evident. Thus, it is common for younger anthropologists, reared on the diet of relativism which the studies mentioned above exemplify, to be shocked by discovering the old chestnuts of traditional anthropology in their fieldwork just when they had been convinced that these were merely antique illusions.[3]

The dilemma that this particular history reveals is, in fact, typical of the subject matter of anthropology as a whole. What happens is that, first of all, some cross-cultural regularities are recognized: the incest taboo, for example. These lead to quick explanations in terms of the evolution of culture and their 'function' for society as a whole, for individual well-being, or for reproductive success. These explanations are then shown to be based on a gross exaggeration of the unity of the phenomena to be explained. Then explanation is abandoned altogether and declared impossible, leaving anthropologists and, even more, the wider public with the feeling that the original question has been more evaded than faced. In this way the very idea of the possibility of anthropology is destroyed.

THE EPIDEMIOLOGICAL APPROACH TO REPRESENTATIONS

The aim of this chapter is to shun such evasion and to sketch a theoretical model applied to a particular case – in other words, to see how a possible explanation might be framed in the case of a particular example of one of these 'obvious' regularities, the varied but similar peculiar relationships of the mother's brother and the sister's son in different societies. We want to do this without either exaggerating the unity of the phenomenon or avoiding the problems discussed above concerning misplaced realism, which recent theoretical criticism has well illuminated.

What is involved in explaining a cultural phenomenon? Here is a way of framing the question. All members of a human community are linked to one another across time and space by a flow of information. The information is about themselves, their environment, their past, their beliefs, their desires and fears, their skills and practices. The flow has rapid and slow currents, narrow rivulets and large streams, confluence and divisions. All the information in this flow is subject to distortion and decay. Most of it is about some here-and-now situation and does not flow much beyond it. Still, some of it is more stable in content and more widely distributed, being shared by many or even most members of the community. When anthropologists talk of culture, they refer to this widely shared information.

What explains the existence and contents of culture in the social flow of information? An answer of a sort is provided by modern interpretive anthropology, which aims to show that the elements of a culture (or of a cultural subsystem) cohere and constitute an integrated world-view (see in particular Geertz 1973). This is not the approach we favour. Without denying the insightfulness of such interpretive scholarship and the relative systematicity of culture, we are among those who have argued that this systematicity is often much greater in the anthropologists' interpretation than in the culture itself (e.g. Leach 1954, Bloch 1977, Sperber 1985a) and therefore is exaggerated (as is acknowledged by James Boon (1982: 3–26), who speaks approvingly of the 'exaggeration of cultures'). More important, even if cultures were as systematic as claimed, this would fall far short of explaining the spread and stability of these coherent wholes, unless one were to take as given that there are factors and mechanisms in the flow of information that somehow promote systematicity. Rather than assuming their existence, we favour studying the factors and mechanisms actually at work in the spread and stabilization of cultural phenomena and leaving as an open question the degree and manner in which they may indeed promote systematicity.

Our explanatory approach to this flow of information in society is that of the 'epidemiology of representations' (Sperber 1985b, 1996). It is naturalistic – that is, it aims at describing and explaining cultural phenomena in terms of processes and mechanisms, the causal powers of which are wholly grounded in their natural (or 'material') properties. More specifically, the kind of naturalistic explanation of cultural phenomena we favour invokes two kinds of small-scale processes: psychological processes within individuals and physical, biological and psycho-physical interactions between individuals and their immediate environment (including interactions with other individuals) that we call 'ecological' processes. Typically, the scale of the processes invoked is much smaller than that of the cultural phenomena described and explained in terms of them. It is the articulation of large numbers of these microprocesses that allows one to redescribe and explain cultural macrophenomena. This contrasts with more standard social science accounts that explain cultural macrophenomena in terms of other social and cultural macrophenomena.[4]

We view, then, the flow of information as a natural process occurring in the form of causal chains of microevents that take place both in individual mind/brains and in the shared environment of the individuals involved. Inside minds, we are dealing with processes of perception, inference, remembering, decision and action planning, and with the mental representations (memories, beliefs, desires, plans) that these processes deploy. In the environment, we are dealing with a variety of behaviours, often involving artefacts, and in particular with the production and reception of public representations that can take the form of behaviours such as gestures or utterances, or of artefacts such as writings. We call these representations 'public' because, unlike mental representations, they occur not within brains but in the shared environment of several persons. Thus not just discourse addressed to a crowd but also words whispered in someone's ear are 'public' in the intended sense. Mental events cause public events, which in turn cause mental events, and these chains of alternating mind-internal and mind-external events carry information from individual to individual. A simple example is provided by a folktale, in which the main mental events are those of comprehension, remembering, recall and speech planning, and the main public events are tellings of the tale. What makes a particular story a folktale is the fact that repeated sequences of these mental and public events succeed in distributing a stable story across a population over time.

All these events taking place inside and outside individual minds are material events: changes in brain states on the one hand and changes in the immediate environment of individuals on the other. As material events, they possess causal powers and can be invoked as causes and effects in naturalistic causal explanations. They differ in this respect from the abstract meanings invoked in interpretive explanation (see Sperber 1985a: Ch. 1). That meanings can be causes is contentious, and what kind of causal power they might have, if any, is obscure (see Jacob 1997). For instance, attributing to a folktale a meaning that coheres with, say, basic values of the culture in which it is told may, in a way, 'make sense' of the tale, but it does not come near explaining its distribution and hence its existence as a folktale in that particular culture.

It could be objected that the microevents invoked in an epidemiological approach are at the level of individual minds and behaviours. How, then, can their study help explain cultural macrophenomena that exist not on an individual but on a societal scale? We have already suggested that these macrocultural phenomena are made up, at a microscopic level, of these causally linked microevents. To this it is sometimes objected that the vast majority of these microevents cannot be observed: anthropologists will never witness more than a very small sample of the public microevents involved, and mental events cannot be observed at all. Here, however, the comparison with medical epidemiology should help dispose of this objection.

Epidemiological phenomena such as epidemics are macrophenomena occurring at the level of populations, but they are made up of microphenomena of individual pathology and interindividual transmission. In most cases individual pathological processes are not directly observable and are known only through symptoms and tests, while the vast majority of microevents of disease transmission go unobserved. This, however, has been a challenge rather than an impediment to the development of medical epidemiology. In the epidemiology of representations the situation is, if anything, better than in the epidemiology of diseases. Our communicative and interpretive abilities give us a great amount of fine-grained information about the representations we entertain and about the process they undergo, whereas pain and other perceptible symptoms generally provide much coarser and harder-to-interpret information about our pathologies. Also, most events of cultural transmission require the attention of the participants, whereas pathological contagion is typically stealthy. Hence cultural transmission is much easier to spot and observe than disease transmission.

In spite of the limited evidence at its disposal, medical epidemiology has provided outstanding causal explanations of epidemiological phenomena. It has done so only occasionally by following actual causal chains of transmission and much more often by helping to identify the causal factors and mechanisms at work both within and across individual organisms. *Mutatis mutandis*, the task of the epidemiology of representations is not to describe in any detail the actual causal chains that stabilize (or destabilize) a particular cultural representation (although in some cases it is of great historical interest to be able to do so) but to identify factors and processes that help explain the existence and effect of these causal chains. For instance, showing that a particular folktale has an optimal structure for human memory and that there are recurring social situations in a given society in which people are motivated to tell it or to have it told helps explain why the tale is told again and again with little or no distortion of content in that society.

The central question on which an epidemiological approach focuses is what causes some representations and practices to become and remain widespread and relatively stable in content in a given society at a given time.[5] In so framing the question, we depart from the goal of generally explaining all or even most sociocultural phenomena in one and the same way, either as fulfilling a function (a coarse functionalist approach) or as contributing to reproductive success (a coarse sociobiological approach). True, from an epidemiological point of view, all explanations of sociocultural phenomena will have to invoke both mind-external ecological factors linked to the transmission of cultural contents and mind-internal psychological factors linked to the mental representation and processing of these contents. However, the particular factors at play and the way they combine vary with each case (just as, in medical epidemiology, a different combination of organism-internal physiological factors and of organism-external environmental factors characterizes each disease). Because of this multiplicity of co-occurring causes, we aim only at identifying some of the factors that contribute to explaining particular instances. These factors play a causal role only in specific historical and environmental circumstances and therefore can never be sufficient to explain the local cultural forms. Caused in part by the same factors, these forms have recognizable similarities – which we aim to help explain. However, we merely identify a couple of important and recurring factors among many other diverging factors: each cultural form in its full local specifics is therefore unique to its particular historical context.

This, of course, is, first of all, simply to return, though more explicitly and critically, to the general multifactorial explanations that were typical of anthropology before its recent relativist turn. Two things may be new, though. Rather than accepting implicitly some nondescript naturalism or objectivism about kinship, we appeal quite explicitly to naturalistic considerations about evolved, genetically transmitted psychological predispositions. The result of this explicitly naturalistic account is, however, weaker in its predictive pretensions than the type of account found, for example, in Goody's functionalist thesis. There the sister's son's privilege seemed an almost necessary solution to a structural problem found in certain patrilineal societies. Similarly, this solution was to account for the particular form of the institution, for example, the snatching of significant property. According to our more explicitly naturalistic but at the same time more modest account, there are some factors that increase the chances that the sister's-son privilege will stabilize as a cultural form in these societies, and we can expect and not be disturbed by a wide range of unexplained variation in practices because these will always be combined with many other factors and many different histories. We avoid, or so we hope, the too-strong explanations of functionalism, old-style cultural evolutionism, and sociobiology without giving up on causal explanation.

A few simple examples will give an idea of the range of factors that an epidemiological approach would consider relevant and the complex interrelation between mind-internal and mind-external factors. Density of population is a mind-external factor in the stabilization of drumming as a means of communication. The fact that percussion sounds tend to pre-empt human attention is a mind-internal factor in the culturally stabilized uses of percussion instruments. The relative ease with which human memory retains texts with specific prosodies is a mind-internal factor in the stabilization of various forms of poetry; familiarity with specific, historically evolved poetic forms is a mind-internal factor in the acceptability, learnability and, therefore, chances of cultural stabilization of new poetic works. The effectiveness of internal-combustion engines for moving vehicles is a mind-external factor contributing to the stabilization of the techniques involved in constructing and maintaining these engines. Untutored human minds do not, however, spontaneously or even easily acquire these techniques; hence the recognition of the effectiveness of internal combustion is a mind-internal motivating factor in the setting up of appropriate institutional teaching without which the relevant technologies would not stabilize. Institutional teaching itself involves a complex articulation of mind-internal and mind-external factors.

As these examples illustrate, both mind-external and mind-internal factors explaining cultural phenomena can pertain just to the natural history of the human species and its environment or involve also the sociocultural history of the populations involved. On the mind-external side, density of population is a natural factor that is found in all living species but can be modified by cultural factors. Demographic density has a wide variety of cultural effects, the stabilization of drummed communication in some low-density populations being a marginal but obvious illustration. On the mind-external side again, the presence in the environment of vehicles powered by internal combustion engines is a wholly cultural factor – which does not mean that it is non-natural (it is, after all, the product of evolved mental mechanisms exploiting natural laws) – that contributes, among many other sociocultural effects, to the stabilization of the techniques necessary for their construction and maintenance. On the mind-internal side, the tendency of human attention to be pre-empted by percussion sounds, although it can be culturally modified, is basically a natural trait that humans share with other animals. The ability to organize knowledge in a hierarchy of concepts is typically human, and although it is likely to have a strong natural basis it is certainly enhanced by language, writing and formal teaching. Familiarity with specific poetic forms is a wholly cultural trait. This illustrates an important difference, among several, between the epidemiology of diseases and the epidemiology of representations: culture occurs both inside and outside of minds, whereas diseases qua diseases occur only inside organisms.

The epidemiological model therefore does not deny the complexity of the process of human history. It fully recognizes that culture is both in us and outside – that it is not (even remotely) just a matter of human beings with genetically determined mind/brains reacting to diverse environments according to the dictates of their nature. But the recognition of this complexity and of the unique fact that humans are beings who, in a strong and important sense, make themselves, still leaves room for considering, inter alia, the role of factors such as human psychological dispositions resulting from natural evolution. However, just as cultural patterns are never simple phenotypic expressions of genes, they are never simple social-scale projections of the individual mind. Culture is not human mentation writ large. It is, rather, the interaction of psychological dispositions with mind-external factors in a population that can best explain the sporadic recurrence of certain types of behaviours and norms in a whole variety of guises. The inability of other models to do this – an inability common in the social sciences – has left anthropology ill-equipped to explain many of the cross-cultural regularities which have, in the past, rightly fascinated it.

A rich example of the relationship between evolved psychological dispositions, mind-external factor, and cultural phenomena is afforded by the case of language. A common assumption in cognitive psychology is that humans come equipped with a language faculty. This language faculty is neither a language nor a disposition that generates a language in the individual *ex nihilo*, but a disposition to acquire a specific language on the basis of external linguistic inputs. The disposition is assumed to work like this: Infants react differently to sound patterns typical of human speech: they pay particular attention to these sounds, analyse them differently from other sounds, look for special evidence such as speaker's gaze in order to associate meaning with sound, structure meaning in partly preformed ways, test their knowledge by themselves producing speech, and generally develop a competence in the language of their community. That the language acquired by the members of a community depends on the public linguistic productions encountered in this community is a truism. However, the languages found in all human communities depend on the psychological disposition that individuals bring to the task of language acquisition. Generally, human languages have to be learnable on the basis of this disposition. More specifically, phonetic, syntactic and semantic forms are more likely to stabilize when they are more easily learnable. All so-called natural human languages – that is, languages the evolution of which is essentially the output of spontaneous collective linguistic activity – will therefore exhibit structural features that make them highly learnable as a first language by humans.

Languages – Chinese, English, Maori and so forth – differ because they have different histories, with a variety of factors such as population movements, social stratification, and the presence or absence of writing affecting these histories in subtle ways. However, these mind-external, place-and-time-specific factors interact in every generation with the language faculty found in every human. It is this interaction that determines the relative stability and the slow transformation of languages and puts limits on their variability. For a variety of socio-historical reasons, topics of conversation, preferred words, socially valued patterns of speech, and so on, vary continuously over time in such a way that every generation is presented with a somewhat different sampling of linguistic inputs, to which it reacts, in the acquisition process, by unconsciously bringing about minor changes in the underlying grammar. Generally, whereas day-to-day cultural changes in language use may introduce new idiosyncrasies and difficulties such as hard-to-pronounce borrowed words, the language-learning disposition operating at the generational timescale pulls the mental representations of these inputs toward more regular and more easily remembered forms. For instance, the more difficult phonology of borrowed words or the more difficult semantics of meanings stipulated as part of sophisticated theories are likely to be normalized by language learners in the direction of easier forms. This determines a slow evolution of languages that is constrained both by the necessity of intergenerational communication and by the universal constraints of language acquisition.

The case of language learning, therefore, illustrates how the existence of a genetically inherited disposition is a factor in the stabilization of cultural forms not by directly generating these forms but by causing learners to pay special attention to certain types of stimuli and to use – and sometimes distort – the evidence provided by these stimuli in specific ways. This, of course, leaves room for much cultural variability. Moreover, dispositions capable of affecting cultural contents may be more or less rigidly constraining, the language-acquisition device envisaged by Chomskyans being on the more constraining side. In general, cultural representations departing from those favoured by underlying dispositions, though possible, do not stabilize as easily. In the absence of other stabilizing factors counterbalancing the dispositions (e.g. institutional support), hard-to-learn representations tend to get transformed in the process of transmission in the direction favoured by the dispositions.

The epidemiological approach to culture provides a way of understanding the relationship between psychology and culture that neither denies the role of psychology nor reduces culture to mind. In a nutshell, the idea is that psychological dispositions in general (whether evolved basic dispositions or culturally developed dispositions) modify the probability – and only the probability – that representations or practices of some specific tenor will spread, stabilize and maintain a cultural level of distribution.

How might all this help explain the regularities in the relationship between mother's brother and sister's son in patrilineal societies that are the topic of this chapter? To this we now turn.

APPLYING THE THEORY TO THE MOTHER'S-BROTHER/SISTER'S-SON RELATION

Underlying the theories of the structural-functionalists concerning the mother's-brother/sister's-son relation in patrilineal societies was the assumption that all human beings really reckon kinship bilaterally. This made the occurrence of unilineal rules to form descent groups something which somehow 'went against nature'. Thus Fortes (1969) contrasted the domestic domain, in which relations were governed by biology and natural emotions, with the lineage domain, which was constrained by politico-jural considerations in conflict with this biology. For him, therefore, the claims of the sister's son were a kind of reassertion of underlying bilaterality. Goody, although distancing himself somewhat from the Fortesian formulation, seemed to imply something similar in that the reason the sister's son was being 'cheated' of his inheritance by the patrilineal rule was that in reality he, like the maternal uncle's children, was a true descendant of his mother's parents. The objection to Fortes's and Goody's position, however, has been, as we have seen, that they seemed to assume that people acted in terms of genetic relations rather than in terms of a very different thing, their representation of socially specified relations. But what if there were some indirect causal link between social representations and genetic relations? Then the accusation of naive empiricism might fall away and the Fortes/Goody argument might be partly reinstated. How this might be possible is what much of the rest of this chapter is about.

We begin by noting that support for the structural-functionalists' assumption of the universal bilaterality of kinship seems to come from an unexpected source. This is Hamilton's (1964) neo-Darwinian explanation of kin altruism and its development in sociobiological theory. However, this kind of theory has been rejected out of hand by most social and cultural anthropologists (e.g. Sahlins 1976). It is necessary to outline the theory of kin altruism and why it has been rejected to see if, after all, it might not be used legitimately in favour of the kind of argument implicit in the writings of Goody and Fortes.

The by-now familiar kin-altruism argument can be summarized as follows: genealogical relationships in the strict biological sense exist among all organisms, including humans. The transmission of heritable biological traits through genealogical relationships is what makes natural selection possible. Natural selection favours genes which have the effect, given the environment, of rendering more probable more replications of themselves in future generations. This includes genes that promote the reproduction of the organism in which they are located, genes that promote behaviours favourable to the survival and reproduction of descendants of the organism in which they are located, and also – and this is fundamental to Hamilton's thesis – genes that promote survival and reproduction in yet other organisms which, being genealogically related, are likely to carry copies of the same genes. A gene causing an organism to pay a cost or even to sacrifice itself for the benefit of its lateral kin may thereby increase the number of copies of itself in the next generation, not through the descendants of the cost-paying or self-sacrificing organism (which may thereby lose its chance of reproducing at all) but through the descendants of the 'altruistic' organism's kin, who are likely to carry the very same gene.

The potential contribution of kin altruism to what is known as 'inclusive fitness' favours the emergence of a disposition to helpful behaviour adjusted to the genealogical distance between the altruist and the beneficiary. For such a disposition to exert itself, the organism must have the possibility of discriminating kin from non-kin and, among kin, degrees of relatedness. This does not mean, of course, that the organism must have the conceptual resources to represent genealogical relatedness and its degrees precisely and as such. What it means is that, if the ecology is such that degree of relatedness can, at least roughly, be discriminated thanks to some simple criterion such as smell, appearance or habitat, then a disposition exploiting this possibility may be selected for.

The importance of the theory of kin altruism for evolutionary biology and for the sociobiological study of animal behaviour is not in dispute, but what are its consequences, if any, for the study of human behaviour? At first sight this theory, transposed directly to humans, would predict that the requirements of this altruism should, in humans, favour an instinctually based universal bilateral recognition of kinship. This would be *a priori* support for the structural-functionalists' assumption. Here, however, is where the objections of most anthropologists come in.

These objections are fundamentally two. First, the great variability in kinship systems throughout the globe seems unaccountable in terms of panhuman characteristics. Second, humans live in the world via their representations, and how one gets from genes to representations or norms has simply not been thought through in the sociobiological literature (which has been criticized precisely on this ground by evolutionary psychologists (see Tooby and Cosmides 1992).

The first objection means that the explanation in terms of genes is far too direct. One should note, however, that the sociobiological position not only is compatible with the recognition of some degree of variability but also purports to explain it. The expression of genes is always contingent on environmental factors, and it may be part of the contribution of a gene to the fitness of the organism that it has different phenotypic expressions in different environments. For instance, the sex of many reptiles is determined not directly by their genes but by the temperature at which eggs are incubated, females developing better, it seems, and being more often born in a warmer environment and males in a colder one (Shine, Elphick and Harlow 1995).

Closer to our present concern, Alexander (1979) offers an explanation of both matrilineal inheritance and sister's-son rights in patrilineal societies in terms of uncertainty of paternity. An evolved disposition to favour kin should be sensitive to degrees of doubt or certainty of relatedness. In particular, a man's investment in his putative children should be sensitive to his degree of confidence that he is actually their biological father. If there are reasons that this degree of confidence should be low, then a man's closest relatives in the next generation may well be his sister's children. On this basis, Alexander predicts 'that a general society-wide lowering of confidence of paternity will lead to a society-wide prominence, or institutionalization, of mother's brother as an appropriate male dispenser of parental benefits' (1979: 172). One may accept the premise that there is an evolved disposition to favour kin that is sensitive to confidence in relatedness and yet doubt Alexander's conclusion, in particular regarding the institutionalization of matrilineal inheritance. True, there is ethnographic evidence that confidence in paternity tends, with exceptions, to be lower in matrilineal than in patrilineal society, as the case of the nineteenth-century Nayars illustrates (Gough 1959), but it is most probably even lower in societies which have neither matrilineal nor patrilineal descent groups (Gibson 1986, Stack 1983). Furthermore, a correlation is not sufficient to determine that there is a direct causal relationship, let alone what the direction of such a causal relationship might be.

The ethnographic and historical record shows that matrilineality and patrilineality and related patterns of inheritance are fairly stable systems, with very rare documented examples (such as Barnes 1951) of a society's shifting from one to the other. In contrast, changes in sexual mores toward or away from greater permissiveness and associated lower confidence in paternity are very common and may be caused by rapidly shifting economic, demographic or ideological factors. It cannot be the case, then, that a lowering of confidence in paternity systematically or even frequently leads to the institutionalization of matrilineality. Alexander's claim, therefore, is at best unconvincing. One could, for that matter, argue that the lower confidence in paternity in matrilineal society is an effect rather than (or as much as) a cause of the descent system. When the inheritance system is matrilineal, then a man knows that his heirs will be his sister's children rather than those of his wife. His chances of investing in his wife's children's welfare may be further reduced by rules of separate residence of the spouses such as are often found in matrilineal societies. To the extent that the opportunities for a man to invest resources in his wife's children are limited, it may matter relatively less whether these children are biologically his own, especially if the counterpart of greater paternity doubts is a greater chance of having children with other men's wives. This fits well with the common ethnographic observation that in most matrilineal societies there is less control over the sexual fidelity of women.

Extending Alexander's line of reasoning to the case with which we are concerned here, one would predict that the chances of having institutionalized privileges for the sister's son in an otherwise truly patrilineal system will be greater when paternity doubts are greater (but not great enough to tip the system over toward matrilineality). In this case, however, we know of no evidence of a correlation between institutionalized privileges of sister's son and paternity doubts, let alone a causal link in the hypothesized direction.

The second standard anthropological objection to a biological account implies that, even if we accept that a disposition to Hamiltonian kin altruism is biologically advantageous and therefore likely to have somehow evolved (something which is clearly plausible), it is not clear at all what would follow regarding cultural norms of human behaviour. The answer is probably nothing directly and unconditionally, since dispositions to behaviour need not actually lead to behaviour, let alone to culturally codified behaviour; they may be offset or inhibited in many ways. Moreover, assuming that a disposition is not inhibited, it still need not be reflected in a cultural norm. In most human society, for instance, the disposition to use, under certain conditions, an eyebrow flash as a sign of recognition is both uninhibited and culturally uncodified (see Eibl-Eibesfeldt 1975). Should we, then, as do most cultural and social anthropologists, simply forget about all this biological stuff and, along with the theologians and philosophers of old, recognize that the categorical uniqueness of human beings frees them completely from animality?

The epidemiological approach offers a way of avoiding this type of dismissal while taking into account what is valuable in the objections. Let us accept, as a hypothesis, that there is an evolved disposition to try to differentiate people in a way sensitive to their degree of genealogical relatedness to self. It is most unlikely that such a disposition would be such as to cause the individual to seek actual genealogical information. It would be rather a disposition merely to seek whatever available information might indicate relatedness to self.[6] Now, such a disposition would favour the cultural stabilization of systems of representation providing for such ego-centred differentiation without determining their exact nature. The disposition would not be the source of these representations; these would arise as part of the process of distribution of ideas and practices – the historical dialectic of thought and communications, so to speak – and its interaction with the individual cognitive development of the members of every new generation. The epidemiological approach seeks factors explaining the transformation and stabilization of representations in the process of their transmission, including biological factors. It does not pretend, as might a classical sociobiological approach, that these biological factors somehow generate the representations or that culturally sanctioned behaviours are phenotypic expressions of genes.

One prediction that would follow from the hypothesis we are considering is that individuals would tend to show interest in evidence of relatedness, whether or not culturally codified. For instance, if a single kinship category included full sibling, half-sibling and more distant relatives, with the same cultural norms of behaviour vis-à-vis all, individuals would nevertheless tend to differentiate both cognitively and behaviourally between the different types of individual falling into this category (see e.g. Bloch 1998). This further interest could be carried out individually without being particularly culturally condoned, as we have just envisaged, or it could contribute to the stabilization of further cultural representations (e.g. folk theories, tales, alternative or complementary terminologies for kin) drawing finer-grained distinctions than the basic kinship-terms system. In other words, whenever representations involving classifications and norms which distinguish kin in terms of closeness appeared amid the babble and multiplicity of other representations caused either by individual imaginations and circumstances or by more general socio-historical circumstances, these particular representations would seem strangely 'right', 'attractive', 'natural', or 'obvious' to people. This would be the case without individuals being at all sure why these representations had these qualities, and even if they gave reasons these reasons would often be merely *post hoc* rationalizations.

Assuming this general framework, we would make the following predictions. In unilineal systems where transmission of rights and goods and generally helpful behaviour creates an inequality of treatment among individuals who are equally closely related to ego and therefore goes against the predisposition in question, there should be a general, nondeterministic tendency to compensate for this imbalance. Norms or institutions capable of playing, in such a system, a compensatory role would simply stand a greater chance of stabilizing than in systems where the imbalance did not exist in the first place. The special rights of the sister's son found in some patrilineal cultures could well be a case in point.

The relationship between biological disposition and cultural norm that we are envisaging in this case is one between a biological causal factor that is obviously not sufficient and maybe not necessary, but such as to render more probable the emergence and stabilization of norms of the type in question. We emphasize that this more sophisticated naturalism makes, in this case, weaker claims than the common-sense naturalism of anthropologists such as the nineteenth-century cultural evolutionists and Malinowski, Radcliffe-Brown, Fortes and Goody. According to their common-sense naturalism, there are natural kinship facts that people are somehow aware of and that guide their sentiments and behaviours. This makes a strong universalistic claim about human cognition, emotion and behaviour, which are taken to be neatly attuned to natural facts. If these classical claims appear misleadingly weaker and more acceptable than those we are tentatively considering here, it is only because they are made, for the most part, implicitly, whereas we have tried to spell out a possible naturalistic approach.

According to the approach we are considering, there are indeed biological facts and, in particular, genealogical relationships. These, however, need not be cognized as such by people. A predisposition to attend to reliable correlates of these relationships cognitively, emotionally or behaviourally in one or several of a multiplicity of possible ways is likely to have evolved in many species, including the human species. In humans, this attention to relatedness encounters a wealth of relevant cultural inputs. More specifically, developing children, searching their environment for evidence of relatedness to others, find kinship terms ('kinship' now in the cultural rather than the biological sense), people identified as related to them by means of these terms, do's and don'ts relating to kinship categories, folk theories, etc. Because of their evolved disposition, they attend to this information or even seek it, retain it, use it to guide their behaviour, and become, in turn, transmitters of such information.

At this stage we seem to be just defending a weakened, updated and explicit version of the implicit or less explicit naturalistic claims of Fortes and Goody regarding the mother's-brother/sister's-son relation in certain patrilineal societies. In fact, given the sweeping and careless way in which these claims have been dismissed, this is worth doing in any case. We are defending them, however, in a way that is not contradicted by the very real uniqueness of each case. Furthermore, in contrast to sociobiologists assuming a fairly direct connection between genes and culture, we claim only an indirect relationship of genetically favoured receptivity to specific information, favouring in turn the stabilization of cultural representations of a more or less specific tenor.

WHY RITUALIZED TRANSGRESSION?

From Junod to Goody, ethnographers have stressed the transgressive style in which the sister's son's rights are exerted. This may take many forms, from ritualized insults among the BaThonga to ritualized snatching of meat among the Lo Dagaba. Why should it be so? The general approach we are proposing might help us understand not just the recurrence of the recognition of the subsidiary rights of the sister's son in his mother's brother's property but also the ritualized transgressions so often involved in exerting those rights.

From a cultural-epidemiological point of view, cultural norms (such as the norm that authorizes a Lo Dagaba man to snatch meat from his mother's brother) are just a kind of representation that is widely distributed in a population through various processes of transmission. What makes them norms is the fact that they represent the way things are required or allowed to be. In the social science literature, norms are mostly envisaged as causes of behaviours conforming to them. However, norms play other causal roles which may be no less important. In particular, they serve to confer approval or blame on behaviours attributed to oneself or to others or just on behaviours that occur very rarely, if at all, but the very possibility of which captures the imagination and defines the limits of what is acceptable. In most societies, for instance, norms against cannibalism are much more important as a topic of narrative and conversation than as a guide for behaviour. It would be interesting to know how much the norm permitting a sister's son to take his mother's brother's goods in one or another ritualized way results in actual taking of goods with significant economic effects, as opposed to being a topic of conversation with occasional symbolic enactments, serving to define social roles more than to reallocate economic resources. Alas, the literature does not seem to offer the kind of data that would answer this question. Moreover, things are likely to differ in this respect across different societies and times.

Norms are not just causes of behaviours but also effects of behaviours. Their spreading is caused by the different types of behaviours that they promote. In other words, norms are cultural to the extent that they are distributed by causal chains in which mental representations of the norms and public behaviours (including public statements of the norm) alternate. Again, it would be interesting to know how much a norm such as that permitting goods-snatching is maintained by actual acts of snatching and how much by statements of and about the norm.

Both universal and culture-specific factors may contribute to the acceptability and attractiveness of a norm and therefore to its chance of reaching, in a given socio-historical situation, a cultural level of distribution. Whatever the extent to which a norm permitting ritualized transgression causes behaviours that conform to it, the cultural stability of the norm is a sign of its psychological acceptability and attractiveness – which have to be explained. Here we propose some considerations relevant to such an explanation.

Suppose that there is a type of behaviour that, for different reasons, is simultaneously attractive and unattractive in the same society. As a result, there are, in that society, factors that would favour the stabilization of a norm approving this behaviour and other factors that would favour the stabilization of a norm prohibiting it. Under such conditions, the stabilization of one of the two types of norm is an obvious obstacle to the stabilization of the other, opposite type.

In such a case, things can go in one of three ways. The first possibility is that indeed the stabilization of one norm effectively counteracts factors that would have favoured the stabilization of the other. For instance, religious iconoclastic movements have, in different societies, effectively suppressed any type of image even though receptivity to iconic representations, we assume, was still psychologically present and would otherwise have favoured the cultural approval of image production. Here a psychological disposition, although present, fails to favour any direct cultural expression. The second possibility is that the factors favouring opposite norms end up stabilizing some compromise norm, as when images are accepted and even encouraged but only with religious themes. Then there is a third possibility, in which the stabilization of one norm contributes to the stabilization of a well-contained, ritualized form of the opposite norm. One norm dominates, but the other norm applies in clearly insulated circumstances. This state of affairs may actually contribute to the stability of the dominant norm by highlighting the exceptional character of its occasional violation. Thus Bloch (1987) has argued that the sexual chaos expected at certain stages of Malagasy royal rituals must be seen as 'scene setting' for the extreme domestic order dramatized in the next stage.

The behaviour studied by Goody might well be such a case of a potential conflict of norms that results in the stabilization of two sharply contrasting cultural norms caused by very different factors. One, patrilineal descent and inheritance, is wholly dominant, while the other, the rights of the sister's son, takes the form of an authorized transgression with ritual aspects, the very transgressive character of which contributes to the stabilization of the dominant patrilineal norm. This suggestion is, of course, reminiscent of a line of argument famously initiated by Gluckman (1954) and developed by the Manchester school, in particular in the work of Victor Turner (1969). What the epidemiological approach does and the Gluckman-type explanation does not, however, is seek to explain the macrocultural fact of the asymmetrical equilibrium between a dominant norm and its authorized or even prescribed transgression in terms of factors affecting the microprocesses of cultural transmission.

Given the stabilization of a patrilineal norm (the explanation of which is not the topic of this chapter) and the persistence of evolved psychological factors favouring investment of resources in all close kin, whether patrilineally or matrilineally related, we may expect individuals to welcome expressions of these psychological factors provided that they are not incompatible with the patrilineal norm they have internalized. These psychological factors may find an expression through the informal helping by the mother's brother of his sister's children. Here, however, we are talking of individual attitudes rather than of a culturally sanctioned practice. A cultural practice that acknowledges the rights of one's sister's children would normally go against the patrilineal norm and would be unlikely to stabilize (unless the patrilineal norm itself was in the process of destabilization). Expressing interest in the sister's-son/mother's-brother relationship while highlighting the fact that this relationship does not ground normal, regular rights of sharing or inheritance is a way of reasserting by contrast that very patrilineal norm. More specifically, ritualized transgression practices of the type we are discussing here underscore the out-of-the-ordinary character of a sister's son's rights over his mother's brother's goods and thereby contribute to highlighting the normal character of patrilineal transmission of goods. Thus the combination of the dominant patrilineal norm internalized by all members of the society and the psychological factors favouring all close kin renders people receptive and welcoming to a norm of ritualized expression of sister's-son rights.

The norms and practices of ritualized transgression that are likely thus to stabilize are 'catchy' because of their psychological rather than because of their economic effects. These are first and foremost 'symbolic' practices that need not have any significant – let alone any major – effect regarding the actual allocation of resources between direct and lateral descendants. This is a further contrast between the epidemiological account we are sketching here and any sociobiological account that would explain such practices in terms of their putative effects, through reallocation of economic resources, on social stability or biological fitness.

All that we have said, of course, does not amount to a comprehensive explanation of the particular forms of the sister's-son's privileges in any one of the societies discussed by so many ethnographers, and it is important to understand why. There are two reasons for this – besides the very sketchy character of our attempt. First, we have relied on the hypothesis that there is an evolved human disposition that is aimed at modulating behaviour in a way sensitive to degrees of biological relatedness, but this hypothesis is based on speculation, however well-motivated, more than on conclusive hard evidence. Secondly, we are not offering an explanation for why, for example, Lo Dagaba sister's sons behave in precisely the way they do. Indeed, we think a unifactorial or bifactorial explanation of such an ethnographic datum would inevitably be insufficient. Actual cultural practices, as performed by specific individuals at a given time, are embedded in the socio-historical processes that have distributed, stabilized and transformed cultural representations and practices in the population to which these individuals belong. Each of these historical flows is unique. These processes are influenced by many types of factor evolved psychological predispositions being only one of them. Mostly, cultural processes are influenced by other cultural processes. People's behaviour, in particular their conformity or nonconformity to norms, is guided by the representations they have of the world rather than by the way the world is. People's representations are influenced in several ways by the phenomena they are about, but they are influenced also – and to a greater extent in most cases of interest to anthropologists – by other representations, in particular culturally transmitted ones.

All these difficulties and caveats do not mean that we need to abandon generalizing explanations of the kind we have attempted here. In other words, the recognition of the value of the objections to kinship studies of such as Needham and Schneider need not lead to a denial of the relevance of general unifying causes, among which are some universal human dispositions likely to have been naturally selected in the course of evolution. Such a method, precisely because it sets nonabsolute conditions for the expression of general factors, can overcome the difficulty which we highlighted at the beginning of this chapter and which seems to have overwhelmed anthropology. Reasoning in terms of such things as evolved human dispositions has all too often produced too powerful explanations, while the refusal to try to explain obvious though partial recurrences across cultures in the end seems perverse and inevitably leaves anthropological questions to be naively answered by others.

NOTES

1. For Jack Goody.
2. In a way that is typical of the time, the focus was almost exclusively on male roles.
3. Maurice Bloch remembers how, as a student, he was bored with the mother's-brother controversy and convinced that it was an insignificant aberration in the history of the subject but subsequently, during fieldwork in Madagascar, had to listen all night to a drunk endlessly repeating, 'I am your sister's son, and it is your duty to give me a drink.' He then felt haunted by Radcliffe-Brown.
4. Of course, explaining cultural phenomena in terms of microinteractions is not new in anthropology. The work of Fredrik Barth (e.g. 1975, 1987), for example, has been a source of inspiration to the epidemiological approach.
5. How stable do representations have to be to count as 'stable'? From the epidemiological viewpoint, there is no expectation that there will be a neat bipartition, among all representations that inhabit a human population, between individual representations that never stablilize in the community on the one hand, and cultural representations that are transmitted over time and social space with relatively little modification on the other. We expect, on the contrary, to have a continuum of cases between the idiosyncratic and the widely cultural. This viewpoint differs quite radically from the memetic approach to culture of Richard Dawkins and others (e.g. Dawkins 1976, Blakemore 1999), for which memes are true replicators and other mental contents are not. One might wonder, then, when a representation is stable enough to be seen as a cultural representation. We argue, against that very question, that, from an anthropological point of view, representations are best viewed as more or less cultural depending on the breadth, duration and stability of their distribution.
6. Hirschfeld (1984) can be read as suggesting a similar approach and insisting, quite rightly, that an essential relatedness and not just any kind of relatedness is aimed at, but his description of this kind of relatedness in terms of a 'natural resemblance' seems to us inadequate.

REFERENCES

Alexander, R. 1979. *Darwinism and Human Affairs*, Seattle: University of Washington Press.

Barnes, J. 1951. 'Marriage in a Changing Society'. Rhodes-Livingstone Paper.

Barth, F. 1975. *Ritual and Knowledge among the Baktaman of New Guinea*, New Haven: Yale University Press.

——. 1987. *Cosmologies in the Making: A Generative Approach to Cultural Variation in New Guinea*, Cambridge: Cambridge University Press.

Blakemore, S. 1999. *The Meme Machine*, Oxford: Oxford University Press.

Bloch, M. 1977. 'The Past and the Present in the Present', *Man*, n.s. 12: 279–92.

——. 1987. 'The Ritual of the Royal Bath in Madagascar: The Dissolution of Death, Birth and Fertility into Authority', in D. Cannanine and S. Price (eds), *Rituals of Royalty: Power and Ceremonial in Traditional Societies*, Cambridge: Cambridge University Press.

——. 1998. 'Commensality and Poisoning', in A. Mack (ed.), *Food: Nature and Culture*, Social Research 66 (1).

Boon, J. 1982. *Other Tribes, Other Scribes: Symbolic Anthropology in the Comparative Study of Cultures, Histories, Religion and Texts*, Cambridge: Cambridge University Press.

Cavalli-Sforza, L. and M. Feldman. 1973. 'Cultural versus Biological Inheritance: Phenotypic Transmission from Parents to Children (a Theory of the Effect of Parental Phenotypes on Children's Phenotypes), *American Journal of Human Genetics* 25: 618–37.

Collier, J. and S. Yanagisako. 1987. 'Towards a Unified Analysis of Gender and Kinship', in *Gender and Kinship*, Stanford: Stanford University Press.

Dawkins, R. 1976. *The Selfish Gene*, Oxford: Oxford University Press.

Eibl-Eibesfeldt, I. 1975. *Ethnology: The Biology of Behavior*, New York: Holt, Rinehart and Winston.

Fortes, M. 1953. 'The Structure of Unilineal Descent Groups', *American Anthropologist* 55: 17–41.

Geertz, C. 1973. *The Interpretation of Cultures*, New York: Basic.

Gibson, T. 1986. *Sacrifice and Sharing in the Philippine Highlands*, London: Athlone.

Gillison, G. 1993. *Between Culture and Fantasy*, Chicago: University of Chicago Press.

Goody, J. 1959. 'The Mother's Brother and Sister's Son in West Africa', *Journal of the Royal Anthropological Institute* 89: 61–88.

Gluckman, M. 1954. *Rituals of Rebellion in South-East Africa*, Manchester: Manchester University Press.

Gough, K. 1959. 'The Nayars and the Definition of Marriage', *Journal of the Royal Anthropological Institute* 89: 23–34.

Hamilton, W. 1964. 'The Genetical Theory of Social Behavior', *Journal of Theoretical Biology* 7: 1–52.

Hirschfeld, L. 1984. 'Kinship and Cognition', *Current Anthropology* 27: 217–42.

Jacob, P. 1997. *What Minds Can Do*, Cambridge: Cambridge University Press.

Jamous, R. 1991. *La Relation frère-soeur*, Paris: EHESS.

Junod, H. 1912. *Life of a South African Tribe*, Neuchâtel: Attinger.

Kuper, A. 1982. 'Lineage Theory: A Critical Retrospect', *Annual Review of Anthropology* 11: 71–95.

Laland, K. and G. Brown. 2002. *Sense and Non-sense: Evolutionary Perspectives on Human Behaviour*, Oxford: Oxford University Press.

Leach, E. 1954. *Political Systems of Highland Burma*, London: Bell.

———. 1955. 'Polyandry, Inheritance, and the Definition of Marriage', *Man* 55: 182–6.

Needham, R. 1971. 'Remarks on the Analysis of Kinship and Marriage', in R. Needham (ed.), *Rethinking Kinship and Marriage*, London: Tavistock.

Radcliffe-Brown, A. 1924. 'The Mother's Brother in South Africa', *South African Journal of Science* 21: 542–55.

Rivers, W. 1924. *Social Organisation*, London: Kegan Paul.

Rosaldo, M. 1980. *Knowledge and Passion*, Cambridge: Cambridge University Press.

Sahlins, M. 1976. *The Use and Abuse of Biology*, London: Tavistock.

Schneider, D. 1984. *A Critique of the Study of Kinship*, Ann Arbor: University of Michigan Press.

Shine, R., M. Elphick and P. Harlow. 1995. 'Sisters Like it Hot', *Nature* 378: 451–2.

Sperber, D. 1985a. *On Anthropological Knowledge*, Cambridge: Cambridge University Press.

———. 1985b. 'Anthropology and Psychology: Towards an Epidemiology of Representations' (Malinowski Memorial Lecture, 1984), *Man* n.s. 20: 73–89.

———. 1996. *Explaining Culture: A Naturalistic Approach*, Oxford: Blackwell.

Stack, C. 1983. *All our Kin: Strategies for Survival in a Black American Community*, New York: HarperCollins.

Tooby, J. and L. Cosmides. 1992. 'The Psychlogical Foundations of Culture', in J. Barkow et al. (eds), *The Adapted Mind: Evolutionary Psychology and the Generation of Culture*, New York: Oxford University Press.

Turner, V. 1969. *The Ritual Process*, London: Routledge.

Viveiros de Castro, E. 1992. *From the Enemy's Point of View*, Chicago: University of Chicago Press.

INDEX